外国留学生汉语短期速成
A Short Intensive Course tor Foreign Students

新 闻 汉 语 导 读
A Guide to Reading Chinese Newspapers

编　著　施光亨　　王绍新
英文翻译　熊文华　　梁　骁

华语教学出版社
北　京

First Edition   1998

ISBN 7-80052-633-X
Copyright 1998 by Sinolingua
Published by Sinolingua
24 Baiwanzhuang Road, Beijing 100037, China
Printed by China Film Press Printing House
Distributed by China International
Book Trading Corporation
35 Chegongzhuang Xilu, P. O. Box 399
Beijing 100044, China

Printed in the People's Republic of China

前　　言

　　《新闻汉语导读》旨在帮助外国学生培养和提高阅读中文报纸的能力和技巧。它可作学校的教材,供学完汉语基本语法、掌握2500 个左右词语的学生使用;也可供同等水平的汉语自学者使用。这次出版的 1998 年本主要考虑了短期汉语学习者的特点和需要。

　　1991 年我们在日本任教期间,编写了一本《新闻汉语导读》,蒙日本著名汉语学者、东京外国语大学中国语科主任奥水优教授支持,担任本书监修,并热情推荐由东方书店出版了日语注译本。教材出版以后,从传来的信息看,似乎还很受日本汉语教学界朋友们的欢迎,后来果然逐年收到东方书店寄来的新印本。1992 年回国以后,觉得本书的编写思路和体例在国内还是首次,还值得在对外汉语教材的百花园里供同仁们品评,这个想法得到了北京语言学院出版社朋友们的支持,于是加以增修,1993 年 5 月便出版了新的英语注译本,以后连续印刷了三次;其中 1996 年 10 月本曾作过个别的修订。离初次印刷的时间已经过去好几年了,中国国内的改革、开放在深化、扩展,经济建设和社会发展取得了巨大的成就,作为新闻教材应该给人以新的信息,由此就萌生了编写新本的想法;不过这次编写的是供短期速成汉语教学使用的。编者在日、英语注译 的初版本中曾说过,新闻的时效性和教材的稳定性永远是一对矛盾,为此,我们曾努力从语言教学的角度出发,注重新闻汉语的常用词语和句式。这次编写新版本的时候,我们欣喜地发现,原来选择的词、语、格式并没有多大变化。因此,本书从大格局来

1

说,也一仍其旧。中国社会稳定,政策连续,有些语言材料也没有必要强予更换。书名也沿用原来《新闻汉语导读》的名字,以示其渊源。用"新闻"二字也有利于区别报刊、广播中其他的语言材料。

原书的前言有一段是说明本书的思路和使用方法的,现摘述于下:

新闻语言是语言诸文体中的一种。新闻语言知识水平和实践能力的提高,当然离不开一般语言知识和能力的基础,但是它又有自身的特殊风格和常用的词、语、格式。不少语言学习者在学习结束后,将要从事外交、商贸、新闻等职业,阅读报纸,从中获取有关的信息和动态,是他们的重要工作内容。为此,在他们学习期间有必要给予专门训练和培养。对一般语言学习者来说,经常阅读以目的语的文字出版的报纸,也有利于学习和掌握此种语言。因为,报纸每天刊登的大量语言材料,为读者展示了广阔的,极为现实、生动的社会文化背景,同时也及时地提供着语言的最新变化和发展。所以,报纸是学习语言的极好材料。新闻汉语教学历来为中国和世界汉语教学界所重视。

不少正在使用的同类教材大多采用"文选式",以选取报上的整篇材料作为中心课文,配以注释和练习。考虑到初学者一开始接触整段的新闻材料可能遇到的困难,我们编写了这本《导读》。本书把重点放在新闻汉语中常用的词、语格式上,全书按新闻内容分为若干专题。每个专题由四部分组成:一、词语和句子。这部分列出与本专题有关的词、语、格式,配以相关的句子。这是各专题的主要部分,或者说基础部分。二、阅读短文。这部分安排了2至3则短文。这些短文内容比较完整,语言上力求展示上述词、语、格式和句子在成段新闻材料中的面貌。这是各专题的扩展部分。三、练习。练习仍以掌握词、语、格式为重点,课堂教学如有余时,可找到最新出版的报上的同类材料来阅读,作为本书练习的补充。四、附在每个专题后面的小知识。包括读报常识、与本专题有关的词语和背景材料,目的在于帮助学习者理解正文内容,扩充相关知识。从上述安排中,不难看出本书的要旨在"导"。编者希望这样一种设计能为新闻汉语学习者提供一条从"渐入佳境"到"豁然开朗"的路子。有了本书提供的初步语言基础,在打开中文报纸时,不致有如一下子进入原始森林、不辨方向的迷误,或似突然来到繁花似锦的胜地,目不暇给而不知所取的惶惑。这是一条全新的路子,筚路蓝缕,尚望识者教正。

本书的句子和短文多数都采自《人民日报》,少量来自其他报纸的另行标明,如"光明"为《光明日报》,"海外"为《人民日报·海外版》,等等。

1997 年 10 月,北京

Preface

A GUIDE TO READING CHINESE NEWSPAPERS is a textbook intended to assist foreigners in developing and improving their ability to read Chinese newspapers. It can be used in a classroom setting with students who have studied basic Chinese grammar and mastered a vocabulary of approximate 2,500 words; it can also serve as a teach-yourself tool for learners who have reached the equivalent Chinese level. This new edition of 1998 mainly meets the needs of short-term learners of Chinese.

While we were teaching Chinese in Japan in 1991, we compiled a textbook of the same title. The production of the book was greatly supported and even supervised by Professor Masaru Koshimizu, a well-known Japanese scholar of Chinese and head of the Faculty of Chinese Language at Tokyo University of Foreign Studies. On his recommendation, the Toho-Shoten Co., Ltd. (Tongfang Shudian) published the Japanese edition. According to feedback, it seems that the book was well received by the friends in the Chinese teaching circles in Japan, and later we really received a copy of the reimpression sent out by Tongfang Shudian every year. We returned to China in 1992 and thought that the maiden design and layout of the book were worth being appraised by colleagues in the field of teaching Chinese as a foreign language. Our idea was supported by friends at the Beijing Language and Culture University Press. So we enlarged and revised the book and published a new

5

English edition in May 1993. This edition was reprinted three times in succession. We made only a few revisions for the edition of October 1996.

Now several years have passed since its first impression. China's reform and opening up are deepening and expanding, and great achievements have been made in economic construction and social development. A journalist textbook should provide new information. For this reason, there arose the idea of compiling such a new edition. However, the present new textbook of the same title is devoted to a short-term program of intensive Chinese for foreign students. We said in the first Japanese and English editions that the "newness" of the news and "fixedness" of a textbook are always contradictory. Therefore, we tried our best to place emphasis on words, phrases and set patterns common in journalistic Chinese in order to serve the needs of language teaching. In the course of compiling this new edition, we were happy to find that there was little change needed in the words, phrases and set patterns we had selected. Therefore, the overall pattern remains the same as before. Because of the stable society of China and the continuity of China's policy, there is no need for some language materials to be replaced forcibly. The same title of the new book shows its origin. 新闻 (News) is used to distinguish from other language materials that appear in newspapers and periodicals and broadcasting.

There is a passage in the preface of the first edition introducing the thought of this book and explaining how to use the book. Following are the excerpts:

Journalism has a unique style of language. Although fluency in this specialized language is based on the general knowledge and competence acquired in the language, journalism retains its own style, its commonly used expressions and set patterns. Many language learners will eventually work in fields such as diplomacy, foreign trade, commerce, journalism, etc. ; and newspapers become a valuable part of their jobs, which allows them to obtain pertinent and current information on the latest issues and developments. Therefore, special training in reading newspapers is a necessity. For readers at large, reading newspapers can facilitate learning of that language and help further master the language. Newspapers transmit sociocultural information and recent development in a realistic and vivid way. Furthermore, as any language is a " living organism" with constant changes and developments, newspapers provide readers with such new information. Therefore, newspapers are good material for language learning. Journalistic Chinese teaching has always been a major focus for Chinese teaching circles the world over.

Most journalistic Chinese textbooks are of the "article type", i. e. , the main text being a transcription of newspaper material, with accompanying notes and exercises. For this very reason, this "Guide" will help reduce the difficulties beginners often encounter when reading newspaper articles.

This textbook puts emphasis on the words, phrases and set patterns commonly found in journalistic Chinese. It is divided into parts according to the topics of news content, and each part is further subdivided into four sections:

(1) Words and Sentences: In this section, words, phrases and set patterns related to the topic are listed and followed by sentences. This makes up the main body or basics of each topic.

(2) Reading Passages: This section introduces 2 or 3 short passages. The passages are fairly complete in terms of their content and show how those words, phrases and

sentences listed in the previous section are used in news articles. This makes up the extension of each topic.

(3) Exercises: The emphasis here is placed on the words, phrases and set patterns presented earlier. If time is available, it is recommended to complement the exercises with recently published articles.

(4) Background Information: Following each topic are background information and explanations of words and phrases related to the topic. This will facilitate the students' overall comprehension of both the text and the context.

From the above description, it can be seen that the main purpose of this textbook is "to serve as a guide". The compilers hope this book will gradually lead our learners to mastery of journalistic Chinese, so they will hopefully not "suffer" from the confusion and perplexity that many often experience when reading Chinese newspapers. The new approach awaits correction by the knowledgeable.

Most sentences and passages in this textbook are chosen from the *People's Daily* (《人民日报》), the remainder being from other identified newspapers, for instance, 光明 refers to《光明日报》 (the Guangming Daily), and 海外《人民日报·海外版》(the *People's Daily*, Overseas Edition), etc.

October 1997

Beijing

目　　录
CONTENTS

第一课　访问和会谈
I. VISITS AND TALKS

一、词语和句子

（一）关于访问

1：应……邀请，……对……进行……访问

国事访问　正式访问　友好访问　工作访问

---

(1) 外交部发言人今天下午在记者招待会上宣布：应国家
主席江泽民（Jiāng Zémín）的邀请，德意志联邦共和
国总统罗曼·赫尔佐克（Luómàn Hè'ěrzuǒkè，Roman
Herzog）将于 11 月 18 日对中国进行国事访问。
(1996.11.8)

(2) 中国全国人大常委会委员长乔石（Qiáo Shí），圆满结
束了对伊朗历时 3 天的正式友好访问，今天上午 9 时
15 分（当地时间）乘专机离开德黑兰。
伊朗义长等到机场为乔石一行送行。(1996.11.16)

(3) 应国务院副总理兼外交部长钱其琛（Qián Qíchēn）的

1

邀请，俄罗斯联邦外交部长叶夫根尼 • 马克西莫维奇 • 普里马科夫 （ Yèfūgēnní Mǎkèxīmòwéiqí Pǔlǐmǎkēfū，Yevgeny Maksimovich Primakov ）将于11月17日至19日对中国进行正式访问。(1996.11.8)

(4) 李光耀(Lǐ Guāngyào，Lee Kuan Yew)应中国政府邀请于8月3日抵达青岛，开始对中国进行工作访问。(1996.9.3)

2：邀请……访问，……接受了邀请

---

(1) [库昌(Kùchāng，Kucan)总统]邀请中华人民共和国主席江泽民在方便的时候访问斯洛文尼亚。江泽民主席对此表示感谢，并接受了邀请。(1996.10.20)

(2) 会见时，乔石委员长代表李鹏总理邀请[土耳其总理]埃尔巴坎(Āi'ěrbākǎn，Elbacan)在他方便的时候访问中国。埃尔巴坎感谢李鹏总理对他的访华邀请，他表示将在最短的时间内实现访华。(1996.11.10)

（二）关于会谈

1：友好的气氛　坦率的气氛　亲切友好的气氛

---

(1) 双方在友好的气氛中进行了交谈。(1991.1.27)

(2) 双方在友好、坦率的气氛中广泛交换了看法。(1991.1.8)

(3) 会见是在亲切友好的气氛中进行的。(1996.11.14)

```
2:有助于/有利于/促进了……
```

(1) 这次访问有助于推动日中关系的进一步恢复和发展。(1991.1.9)

(2) 领导人的接触和交谈有利于相互之间的了解,有利于相互关系的发展。(1991.2.28)

(3) 双方高层领导人的经常接触促进了相互了解和友谊。(1996.11.)

```
3:会谈  会见  接受采访
   就……问题举行会谈/交换意见(看法)/进行交谈/
   回答提问
```

(1) (标题)江泽民会见日本客人(1996.11.16)

　　吴仪(Wú Yí)与英国工贸大臣会谈

　　乔石接受德国《商报》记者采访(1996.9.5)

(2) 今天下午,江泽民主席与马里总统科纳雷(Kēnàléi,

Konare)在人民大会堂举行会谈。(1996.9.10)

（3）宾主双方就共同关心的国际和地区问题交换了看法，并取得了广泛的共识。(1996.9.5)

宾主就世界和亚太地区形势、双边关系等问题进行了友好的交谈。(1996.9.5)

（4）双方在友好和建设性的气氛中就双边关系进行了深入讨论。两位外长就两国关系阐述了各自的立场，达成了一些共识。(1996.9.26)

（5）就中美关系、台湾、香港问题、中日关系等问题回答了记者的提问。(1996.9.28)

（三）生　　词

1. 应[邀请]	yìng [yāoqǐng]	on (invitation)；at (the invitation of)
2. 国事访问	guóshì fǎngwèn	state visit
3. 发言人	fāyánrén	spokesman
4. 招待会	zhāodàihuì	reception
5. 委员长	wěiyuánzhǎng	committee chairman
6. 圆满	yuánmǎn	satisfactory
7. 结束	jiéshù	to end，to conclude
8. 历时	lìshí	to take（a period of time）
为期	wéiqī	(to be completed) by a definite date)
9. 专机	zhuānjī	private plane，special plane

10. 议长	yìzhǎng	Speaker
11. 一行	yīxíng	entourage
12. 送行	sòngxíng	to see off
13. 总统	zǒngtǒng	president（of a republic）
14. 方便	fāngbiàn	convenience；convenient
15. 气氛	qìfēn	atmosphere or feel (of a place)
16. 坦率	tǎnshuài	candid，frank
17. 交谈	jiāotán	conversation，talks
18. 广泛	guǎngfàn	wide，widespread
19. 看法	kànfǎ	view，viewpoint
20. 有助于	yǒuzhùyú	to contribute to，to conduce to
21. 有利于	yǒulìyú	be favourable to，be advantageous to
22. 促进	cùjìn	to promote
23. 推动	tuīdòng	to push forward
24. 恢复	huīfù	to restore，to resume
25. 接触	jiēchù	to contact；contact
26. 采访	cǎifǎng	to interview
27. 就	jiù	on；in the light of
28. 提问	tíwèn	to raise a question
29. 工贸大臣	gōngmào dàchén	minister of industrial commerce
30. 共识	gòngshí	common understanding

5

31. 形势 xíngshì situation
32. 双边 shuāngbiān bilateral
33. 建设性 jiànshèxìng constructive
34. 阐述 chǎnshù to expound，to set forth
35. 立场 lìchǎng stand，position

（四）专有名词

1. 德意志联邦共和国 Déyìzhì Liánbāng Gònghéguó　the Federal Republic of Germany
2. 全国人［民代表］大［会］常［务］委［员］会 Quánguó Rén［mín Dàibiǎo］Dà［huì］Cháng［wù］Wěi［yuán］huì　the Standing Committee of the National People's Congress
3. 伊朗 Yīlǎng　Iran
4. 德黑兰 Déhēilán　Teheran
5. 俄罗斯联邦 Éluósī Liánbāng　the Russian Federation
6. 青岛 Qīngdǎo　Qingdao，a city in Shandong Province
7. 斯洛文尼亚 Sīluòwénníyà　Slovenia
8. 土耳其 Tǔ'ěrqí　Turkey
9. 《商报》Shāngbào　*Handelsblatt*（a major German daily financial and business newspaper）
10. 马里 Mǎlǐ　Mali
11. 亚太地区 Yà-Tài dìqū　the Asian-Pacific Region
12. 人民大会堂 Rénmín Dàhuìtáng　the Great Hall of the People

二、阅读短文

(一)

江主席将出访亚洲四国
出席亚太经合组织会议

【新华社北京 11 月 19 日电】 外交部发言人今天在记者招待会上宣布,国家主席江泽民将于 11 月 26 日至 12 月 5 日对菲律宾、印度、巴基斯坦和尼泊尔四国进行国事访问。在此之前,江泽民主席将于 11 月 24 日至 25 日出席在菲律宾举行的亚太经济合作组织第四届领导人非正式会议。

发言人说,江泽民主席访问亚洲四国是对四国国家元首的回访,也是中菲、中印建交以来,中国国家主席首次往访。访问期间,江主席将与四国领导人进行会谈和会见,就双边关系和共同关心的国际和地区问题广泛、深入地交换意见。我们相信,江主席的访问对中国与四国双边关系具有重要历史意义,对维护亚洲地区乃至世界的和平与稳定也将产生积极影响。(1996.11.20)

1. 新华社　　Xīnhuáshè　　the Xinhua News Agency
2. 菲律宾　　Fēilǜbīn　　the Philippines
3. 印度　　　Yìndù　　India
4. 巴基斯坦　Bājīsītǎn　　Pakistan
5. 尼泊尔　　Níbó'ěr　　Nepal
6. 亚太经济合作组织　Yà-Tài Jīngjì Hézuò Zǔzhī
　　　　　　　　the Asian-Pacific Economic
　　　　　　　　Cooperation

（二）

李鹏会见日本时事社社长

【本报北京12月4日讯】 今天下午，国务院总理李鹏在人民大会堂会见以村上政敏（Cūnshàng Zhèngmǐn，Masatoshi Murakami）为团长的日本时事社代表团时表示，希望村上社长此行能增加对中国的了解，同时，加强时事社与新华社的友好合作与业务交流。

会见中，李鹏就中日关系等问题回答了村上政敏的提问。

日本时事社代表团是应新华社的邀请来中国进行访问的。

新华社社长郭超人（Guō Chāorén）、国务院外办副主任吕聪敏（Lǚ Cōngmǐn）会见时在座。

（1996.12.5）

1. 时事社　　　　Shíshìshè　the Jiji News Agency
2. 外(事)办(公室) wài(shì) bàn(gōngshì)
　　　　　　　　　　foreign affairs office

三、练　习

(一)熟读下列词语：

(1) 国事访问　正式访问　友好访问　正式友好访问
　　工作访问　私人访问
　　进行访问　应邀访问

(2) 两国关系　双边关系　友好关系　国际关系

(3) 友好的气氛　坦率的气氛　亲切的气氛　诚挚的气氛

(二)阅读下列标题，注意划线的词语：

(1) 江主席将出访亚洲四国(1996.11.20)
　　圆满结束 对智利(Zhìlì, Chile)共和国的正式访问　李
　　鹏总理抵达巴西(Bāxī, Brazil)访问(1996.11.9)
　　[尼泊尔国王]比兰德拉(Bǐlándélā, Birendra)应中华人民
　　共和国主席江泽民的邀请,对中国进行了为期一周的访
　　问后于 1 日回国。(1996.9.3)

(2) 乔石同土耳其议长会谈　双方认为应把两国友好关系推
　　向新阶段(1996.11.9)
　　中意(Yì, Italy)两国总理举行 会谈(1996.11.12)

(3) 乔石分别与土耳其总统总理会见　希望保持两国高层
　　互访促进双边关系(1996.11.10)
　　陈慕华(Chén Mùhuá)会见日本客人(1996.11.10)

(4) 科特迪瓦(Kētèdíwǎ, Côte d'Ivoire)总统接见上海市政府
　　代表团(1996.11.14)

　　叶选平(Yè Xuǎnpíng)拜会阿盟(Ā[lābó lián]méng, the
　　Arab League)秘书长(1996.11.6)

乔石看望我驻约旦(Yuēdàn，Jordan)使馆人员(1996.11.
12)

（5）［委内瑞拉（Wěinèiruìlā，Venezuela）］卡尔德拉
（Kǎ'ěrdélā，Caldera)总统欢宴李鹏总理　李鹏总理举
行答谢招待会(1996.11.15)

阿根廷（Āgēntíng，Argentina）总统到中国使馆做客
(1996.11.10)

四、小　知　识
BACKGROUND INFORMATION

（一）中国的通讯社 Chinese News Agencies

○ 新华社(Xīnhuáshè)全称新华通讯社(Xīhuá Tōngxùnshè)。
中华人民共和国国家通讯社。总社设北京。向国内各报纸、广播电
台、电视台提供新闻和新闻图片，并用多种语言向国外发布新闻和
新闻图片。

新华社（Xīnhuáshè），short for 新华通讯社（Xīhuá
Tōngxùnshè，Xinhua News Agency），is the national news agency
of the People's Republic of China with its head office in Beijing. Its
service is to provide news and newsphotos for all newspapers，radio
and television stations in China，in addition to releasing news
reports and newsphotos in various languages abroad.

○ 中新社（Zhōngxīnshè）全称中国新闻社（Zhōngguó
Xīnwénshè)。中国以海外华侨报刊为主要发稿对象的通讯社，成立
于 1952 年 10 月 1 日。社址设北京。

中新社（Zhōngxīnshè），short for 中国新闻社（(Zhōngguó
Xīnwénshè，China News Service）was founded on 1st October 1952
with its head office in Beijing. It mainly serves the overseas Chinese
newspapers and periodicals by distributing news reports and

newsphotos.

(二)中国的报纸 Chinese Newspapers

中国的报纸有很多,读者可以从名字上大体了解它们的情况。现简要介绍如下:

There are a great number of Chinese newspapers of which the names often give readers some general information.

中国的报纸可分为全国性、地方性和专业性的三种。全国性报纸中最有权威性的是《人民日报》(Rénmín Rìbào)。它是中国共产党中央委员会的机关报。它的"海外版"以海外读者为对象。全国性报纸中还有《光明日报》(Guāngmíng Rìbào,中共中央书记处主办),它除报道国内外重大新闻外,着重报道教育、科技、卫生、文化、体育等方面的消息和动态。China Daily 是英文报。

Chinese newspapers may be classed as national, local and professional papers. Among the national, the most authoritative one is《人民日报》(Rénmín Rìbào, the *People's Daily*), the organ of the Central Committee of the Communist Party of China. Its overseas edition mainly serves overseas Chinese readers. Other national papers are《光明日报》(Guāngmíng Rìbào, the *Guangming Daily*, directed by the Secretariat of the CPC Central Committee) and the English language paper *China Daily*. Aiming to inform its readers about important national and international news, the *Guangming Daily* places emphasis on developments in education, science, technology, health and culture, as well as sports.

地方性报纸是各行政区内中国共产党领导机关的机关报,常以该行政区的名字命名,如:《北京日报》(Běijīng Rìbào)、《天津日报》(Tiānjīn Rìbào)、《浙江日报》(Zhèjiāng Rìbào)等,也有不以行政区名字命名的,如:《解放日报》(Jiěfàng Rìbào,上海)、《新华日报》(Xīnhuá Rìbào,江苏)、《南方日报》(Nánfāng Rìbào,广东)、《大众日报》(Dàzhòng Rìbào,山东)等。

The local dailies are official papers of the CPC local committees. They are mostly named after the province, municipality or region of the corresponding level, such as 《北京日报》(Běijīng Rìbào, *Beijing Daily*),《天津日报》(Tiānjīn Rìbào, *Tianjin Daily*),《浙江日报》(Zhèjiāng Rìbào, *Zhejiang Daily*). A few dailies are otherwise named, such as 《解放日报》(Jiěfàng Rìbào, *Liberation Daily*, published in Shanghai),《新华日报》(Xīnhuá Rìbào, *New China Daily*, in Jiangsu),《南方日报》(Nánfāng Rìbào, *The South Daily*, in Guangdong),《大众日报》(Dàzhòng Rìbào, *Masses' Daily*, in Shandong).

专业性报纸有的是以读者对象命名的,如:《工人日报》(Gōngrén Rìbào,中华全国总工会主办)、《农民日报》(Nóngmín Rìbào,中共中央农村政策研究室主办)、《解放军报》(Jiěfàngjūn Bào,中央军委主办)、《中国青年报》(Zhōngguó Qīngnián Bào,共青团中央主办)、《中国妇女报》(Zhōngguó Fùnǚ Bào,全国妇联主办)等;有的以业务范围命名,如:《经济日报》(Jīngjì Rìbào,国务院主办)、《科技日报》(Kējì Rìbào,国家科委、国防科工委主办)、《中国教育报》(Zhōngguó Jiàoyù Bào,教育部主办)、《中国体育报》(Zhōngguó Tǐyù Bào,国家体育总局主办)、《国际商报》(Guójì Shāngbào,对外贸易经济合作部主办)等。

Some of the professional papers, as their names suggest, are for readers in different walks of life, such as 《工人日报》(Gōngrén Rìbào, *Workers' Daily*, published by the All-China Federation of Trade Unions),《农民日报》(Nóngmín Rìbào, *Farmers' Daily*, by the Rural Policy Research Center under the CPC Central Committee),《解放军报》(Jiěfàngjūn Bào, *Liberation Army Daily*, by the Central Military Commission),《中国青年报》(Zhōngguó Qīngnián Bào, *China Youth Daily*, by the Central Committee of the Communist Youth League of China),《中国妇女报》(Zhōngguó Fùnǚ Bào, *Chinese Women's Daily*, by the All-China Women's

Federation). Other professional papers are named in the light of different occupations, calling, and trade or interests, such as《经济日报》(Jīngjì Rìbào, *Economic Daily*, by the State Council of the People's Republic of China),《科技日报》(Kējì Rìbào, *Science and Technology Daily*, jointly by the Ministry of Science and Technology and Commission of Science, Technology and Industry for National Defence),《中国教育报》(Zhōngguó Jiàoyù Bào, *China Education Daily*, by the Ministry of Education),《中国体育报》(Zhōngguó Tǐyù Bào, *China Sports Daily*, by the State Sport General Administration of China,《国际商报》(Guójì Shāngbào, *International Commerce*, by the Ministry of Foreign Trade and Economic Cooperation).

晚报有的以主要发行地区的地名命名,如《北京晚报》(Běijīng Wǎnbào)等;有的以地方的别名命名,如:《羊城晚报》(Yángchéng Wǎnbào,广州,别名羊城)、《榕城晚报》(Róngchéng Wǎngbào,福州,别名榕城);有的不以地名命名,如:《今晚报》(Jīn Wǎnbào,天津)、《新民晚报》(Xīnmín Wǎnbào,上海)等。

Of the evening newspapers, some are named after the city where they are published, such as《北京晚报》(Běijīng Wǎnbào, *Beijing Evening*). Others are given a name poetically standing for the city where it circulates, such as《羊城晚报》(Yángchéng Wǎnbào, *Five-Ram City Evening*, in Guangzhou),《榕城晚报》(Róngchéng Wǎngbào, *Banyan City Evening*, in Fuzhou). Still others are otherwise named, for example,《今晚报》(Jīn Wǎnbào, *This Evening News*, in Tianjin),《新民晚报》(Xīnmín Wǎnbào, *New Citizens' Evening*, in Shanghai).

文摘报摘编、刊载其他报刊、图书已经发表的内容,较多地注意知识性和趣味性。

There are also papers of digests devoted to abstracts or summaries of the articles from different newspapers, periodicals or magazines. They are well-circulated for the wide range of knowledge and great delight.

（三）汉语词语的简缩 Chinese Abbreviations

报纸为了以较少的版面容纳较多的信息，常常采用简缩的说法。汉语的绝大多数音节——也就是书面上的"字"——都有意义，这就为报纸的这种需要提供了可能性。方法有：

Abbreviations are often used in newspapers to cover more items of information. The meaningfulness of most Chinese syllables，or characters，makes it possible for writers to use them. The following are the ways to shorten words：

1. 用单音节词代替双音节词，如：

Replace a disyllabic word with the monosyllabic equivalent，e.g.：

抵——抵达	达——达到、到达	离——离开
京——北京	邀——邀请	访——访问

2. 使用简称，如：

Use the shortened forms，e.g.：

中共中央——中国共产党中央委员会

外长——外交部长

亚太地区——亚洲太平洋地区

（本书因使用简称而略去的字用［］标记。中国国家机构的名称，中国各省、市、自治区的名字，体育用语，国际组织名称等方面使用简称的情况，详见有关专题）

(In this textbook the omitted characters of a shortened form are printed between square brackets. The abbreviations for Chinese government organizations，Chinese provinces，cities and regions，terms of sports，and international establishments are explained in the chapters where they appear.)

3. 用数字概括：

Use numerals：

——根据字面概括,如:

—— A numeral is used for the simplification according to the structure of the phrase. e. g. :

二为——为人民服务,为社会主义服务(见第 XI 专题 See chapter XI)

双百——百花齐放,百家争鸣(见第 XI 专题 See chapter XI)

四个现代化——工业现代化,农业现代化,国防现代化,科学技术现代化

——根据意义概括,如:

—— A numeral is used for the simplification according to the meaning of the phrase. e. g.

四项基本原则——坚持社会主义,坚持无产阶级专政,坚持共产党的领导,坚持马列主义、毛泽东思想(见第 III 专题 See chapter III)

一个中心,两个基本点——以经济建设为中心,坚持四项基本原则,坚持改革开放(见第 III 专题 See chapter III)

和平共处五项原则——互相尊重主权和领土完整,互不侵犯,互不干涉内政,平等互利,和平共处(见第 XVI 专题 See chapter XVI)

(四) 国家元首的名称 The Chinese Name for the Head of State

总统(zǒngtǒng):如美国、法国、德国、意大利、埃及等;
　　President:for the head of the USA,France,Germany,Italy,Egypt,etc.

国家主席(guójiā zhǔxí):如中国、朝鲜、老挝等;
　　Chairman of a state:for the head of China,DPRK,Laos,etc.

国务委员会主席(guówù wěiyuánhuì zhǔxí):如古巴、越南等;
　　Chairman of a state council:for the head of Cuba,

Vietnam，etc.

国王（guówáng）：如英国、挪威、瑞典、丹麦、荷兰、沙特阿拉伯、斯威士兰等；

King：for the head of the UK，Norway，Sweden，Denmark，the Netherlands，Saudi Arabia，Swaziland，etc.

天皇（tiānhuáng）：如日本；

Emperor：for the head of Japan

大君（dàjūn）：如锡金；

Maharaja〈great king〉：for the head of Sikkim

教皇（jiàohuáng）：如梵蒂冈；

Pope：for the head of Vatican

大公（dàgōng）：如卢森堡；

Grand duke：for the head of Luxembourg

亲王（qīnwáng）：如摩洛哥；

Prince：for the head of Morocco

埃米尔（āimǐ'ěr）：如卡塔尔、巴林、科威特等；

Emir：for the head of Qatar，Bahrain，Kuwait，etc.

苏丹（sūdān）：如阿曼苏丹国等。

. Sultan：for the head of the Sultanate of Oman，etc.

第二课　会　议
II. MEETINGS

一、词语和句子

（一）关于会议的召开

1：……[于]……在……举行/开幕/召开

---

(1) 中国共产党第十四届中央委员会第六次全体会议,于
 1996 年 10 月 7 日至 10 日在北京举行。(1996. 10.
 11)

(2) 八届全国人大常委会第二十二次会议今天上午在京
 开幕。乔石委员长主持今天上午的全体会议。(1996.
 10. 24)

(3) 为期四天的中国国民党革命委员会第八届中央委员
 会第五次全体会议,今天在北京闭幕。会议选举何鲁
 丽(Hé Lǔlì)为民革第八届中央委员会主席。(1996.
 11. 12)

(4) 国务院今天在京召开全国水利工作会议。(1996. 10.
 26)

> 2：会议由……主持　……主持了会议
> 出（列）席会议的有……　……出（列）席了会议

(1) 出席这次（中共十四届六中）全会的中央委员 181 人，候补中央委员 124 人。中央纪律检查委员会委员和有关方面负责同志列席会议。
全会由中央政治局主持。中央委员会总书记江泽民同志作了重要讲话。（1996.10.11）

(2) 中共中央政治局常委、全国政协主席李瑞环（Lǐ Ruìhuán）主持会议。全国政协副主席……和秘书长……出席了会议。（1996.10.13）

（二）会议的议程

> 1：会议的任务/内容/议题/主题　是……

(1) 这次常委会议的主要任务是学习贯彻中共十四届六中全会通过的《中共中央关于加强社会主义精神文明建设若干问题的决议》。（1996.10.13）

(2) 会议的主要内容是学习贯彻中国共产党十四届六中全会精神。（1996.10.22）

(3) "展望 21 世纪论坛"首次会议的主要议题是：展望 21 世纪的亚洲和中国。（1996.9.5）

(4) 第 13 届国际档案大会的主题是：本世纪末的档案工作……回顾与展望。（1996.9.3）

> 2：学习、讨论…… 　听取、审议……
> 通过…… 　审查、批准……

(1) 会议的中心议题是学习、讨论中共十三届七中会全精神。(1991.1.12)
(2) 本次会议通过了四个法律,初步审议了两个法律草案,还听取和审议了关于减轻农民负担问题等三个报告。(1996.10.30)
(3) 全会审议并通过《关于召开党的第十五次全国代表大会的决议》,确定党的十五大于明年下半年在北京举行。(1996.10.11)

（三）生　词

1. 召开	zhàokāi	to convene，to open
2. 闭幕	bìmù	to close，to conclude
3. 届	jiè	a measure word for meetings，graduating classes，etc.
4. 水利	shuǐlì	water conservancy
5. 主持	zhǔchí	to preside over
6. 列席	lièxí	to attend as a nonvoting delegate
7. 候补	hòubǔ	be an alternate
8. 有关	yǒuguān	concerned，related

9. 负责同志/人	fùzé tóngzhì /rén	comrade or person in charge
10. 政治局	zhèngzhìjú	the Political Bureau; Politburo
11. 总书记	zǒngshūjì	general secretary
12. 秘书长	mìshūzhǎng	secretary-general
13. 议题	yìtí	subject for discussion
14. 主题	zhǔtí	theme，subject
15. 贯彻	ʼguànchè	to carry out
16. 关于	guānyú	about，concerning
17. 精神文明	jīngshén wénmíng	culture and ideological progress
18. 精神	jīngshen	gist
19. 展望	zhǎnwàng	look ahead，look into the future
20. 论坛	lùntán	forum
21. 档案	dàngʼàn	files，archives
22. 听取	tīngqǔ	to listen to
23. 审议	shěnyì	to deliberate and discuss
24. 通过	tōngguò	to adopt，to pass
25. 批准	pīzhǔn	to approve，to ratify
26. 国民经济	guómín jīngjì	national economy
27. 规划	guīhuà	programme，plan
28. 纲要	gāngyào	compendium，programme
29. 草案	cǎoʼàn	draft
30. 减轻	jiǎnqīng	to lighten，to ease
31. 负担	fùdān	burden

32. 确定　　　quèdìng　　　to define，to determine

（四）专有名词

1. [国]民[党]革[命委员会] [Guó]mín[dǎng] Gé[mìng Wěiyuánhuì] the Revolutionary Committee of the Chinese Kuomintang（RCCK）
2. 中国人民政[治]协[商会议] Zhōngguó Rénmín Zhèng [zhì] Xié[shāng Huìyì] the Chinese People's Political Consultative Conference（CPPCC）
3. 中[央]纪[律检查]委[员会] Zhōng[yāng] Jì[lǜ Jiǎnchá] Wěi[yuánhuì] the Central Commission for Discipline Inspection（CCDI）

二、阅读短文

(一)

中华人民共和国主席令
第十九号

　　《中华人民共和国职业教育法》已由中华人民共和国第八届全国人民代表大会常务委员会第十九次会议于 1996 年 5 月 15 日通过,现予公布,自 1996 年 9 月 1 日起施行。

中华人民共和国主席　江泽民
1996 年 5 月 15 日

（二）

　　全国政协今天上午在人民大会堂隆重举行孙中山（Sūn Zhōngshān）先生诞辰（dànchén，birthday）130周年纪念大会。中共中央总书记、国家主席江泽民在会上发表了重要讲话。

　　江泽民、李瑞环、朱镕基（Zhū Róngjī）、荣毅仁（Róng Yìrén）等党和国家领导人出席了会议，并在大会开始前亲切会见了孙中山先生的亲属（qīnshǔ，relatives）和海外来宾，与他们合影（héyǐng，to have a group photo）留念。

　　纪念大会由中共中央政治局常委、全国政协主席李瑞环主持。

　　民革中央主席何鲁丽和台盟中央主席蔡子民（Cài Zǐmín）分别代表民革中央和各民主党派、全国工商联、无党派代表人士、各人民团体先后在纪念大会上讲了话。

　　参加今天纪念大会的领导人还有：……

　　出席今天纪念大会的还有：中直机关和国务院各部委负责同志，中央军委、解放军三总部和各军兵种负责同志，北京市党政军群负责同志，各民主党派、无党派民主人士和全国工商联负责人，孙中山先生的亲属、台港澳同胞、海外侨胞和国际友人，以及首都各界人士等共1万多人。

（1996.11.13）

三、练　习

(一)熟读下列词语：

    (1) 举行会议　召开会议　会议开幕　主持会议　出席会议
        列席会议

    (2) 会议认为　会议指出　会议要求　会议决定　会议召开
        会议强调

    (3) 学习讨论　听取审议　审议通过　审查批准　贯彻执行
        贯彻落实

(二)把下列短文译成外语：

    来自全国各地的中国作家协会四届四次理事(lǐshì, member of an executive council)会的 100 多位理事，听取并审议了中国作协书记处(shūjìchù, secretariat)常务书记张锲(Zhāng Qiè)代表书记处作的关于作协五代会筹备工作的报告，通过了大会议程(草案)、大会主席团组成方案和建议名单，通过了大会秘书长、副秘书长的建议名单。会议认为各项筹备工作仔细扎实，中国作协第五次全国代表大会可以如期(rúqī, as scheduled)召开。(1996. 12. 16)

四、小　知　识
BACKGROUND INFORMATION

(一)中国的国家机构 Chinese State Organizations

    全国人民代表大会：中华人民共和国的最高国家权力机关。代表由选举产生，每届任期五年。每年举行会议一次。常务委员会(常委会)是它的常设机关，对全国人大负责并报告工作。委员长主持常委会的工作。

    全国人民代表大会 (the National People's Congress) is the

supreme organ of state power of the People's Republic of China. The NPC, to which members are elected for a term of five years, meets every year. The Standing Committee headed by the Chairman is a permanent body, responsible and accountable to the NPC.

中华人民共和国国务院(Guówùyuàn):即中央人民政府,是最高国家行政机关,由总理、副总理、国务委员、各部部长和各委员会主任组成。

中华人民共和国国务院(the State Council of the People's Republic of China) is the central people's government, or the supreme administrative organization formed by the premier, vice premiers, state councillors, ministers and chairmen of the commissions.

中国人民政治协商会议:中国共产党领导下的爱国统一战线组织,是实行共产党领导的多党合作和政治协商制度的重要组织机构;设全国委员会(全国政协)和地方委员会(地方政协)。1954年前曾代行同级人民代表大会职权。

中国人民政治协商会议 is the patriotic united front organization under the guidance of the Chinese Communist Party, an important organization through which multiparty cooperation and political consultation led by the Communist Party is ensured. Under the National Committee, it has established local committees at various levels. Before 1954 it functioned as the people's congress at the corresponding level.

中央军事委员会(中央军委):统率全国武装力量。由全国人大选举产生,向全国人大和它的常委会负责并报告工作。

中央军事委员会(中央军委)(the Central Military Commission) commands all armed forces in China. It is elected by the National People's Congress, and responsible and accountable to the NPC and its standing committee.

（二）中国的民主党派和全国工商联 Chinese Democratic Parties and the All-China Federation of Industry and Commerce

中国的民主党派是中国的参政党，共有八个。它们是：

There are eight Chinese democratic parties participating in government and political affairs.

中国国民党革命委员会（Zhōngguó Guómíndǎng Gémìng Wěiyuánhuì）：1948 年 1 月成立。主要是由原国民党中的爱国民主分子组织起来的。

中国国民党革命委员会（the Revolutionary Committee of the Chinese Kuomintang）was founded in January 1948 by the patriots of the former Kuomintang members.

中国民主同盟（Zhōngguó Mínzhǔ Tóngméng）：1941 年成立。成员主要是文教界知识分子。

中国民主同盟（the China Democratic League）was founded in 1941. The majority of its members are the intellectuals in the cultural and educational circles.

中国民主建国会（Zhōngguó Mínzhǔ Jiànguóhuì）：1945 年成立。主要是由原民族资产阶级工商业者组成。

中国民主建国会（the China Democratic National Construction Association）was founded in 1945. The majority of its members are the national bourgeois industrialists and businessmen.

中国民主促进会（Zhōngguó Mínzhǔ Cùjìnhuì）：1945 年成立。成员主要是中小学教育界、文化出版界的知识分子。

中国民主促进会（the China Association for Promoting Democracy）was founded in 1945. The majority of its members are the intellectuals in primary and secondary school, cultural and press circles.

中国农工民主党（Zhōngguó Nónggōng Mínzhǔdǎng，农工党）：1930 年创建。主要成员是医药卫生界和文教知识界的知识分子。

中国农工民主党（the Chinese Peasants' and Workers'

26

Democratic Party) was founded in 1930. Most of the members are the intellectuals in the medical, health, cultural and educational circles.

中国致公党(Zhōngguó Zhìgōngdǎng,致公党):成员主要是归国华侨。

中国致公党(Zhōngguó Zhìgōngdǎng, China Zhi Gong Dang) is mainly formed by the returned overseas Chinese.

九三学社(Jiǔsān Xuéshè,九三):原名"民主科学社(Mínzhǔ Kēxuéshè)",1945 年为纪念反法西斯战争的胜利,定名为"九三学社"。成员主要是文教、科技界的知识分子。

九三学社(九三)(the Jiu San Society) was formerly known as "民主科学社"(the Democratic and Scientific Society), renamed "九三学社" in memory of the victory won in the anti-fascist war in 1945. Many of the members are the intellectuals in the cultural, educational and scientific circles.

台湾民主自治同盟(Táiwān Mínzhǔ Zìzhì Tóngméng,台盟): 1947 年成立。由台湾省的一部分爱国民主人士组成。

台湾民主自治同盟(the Taiwan Democratic Self-Government League) was founded in 1947 by the Taiwanese patriotic democrats.

中华全国工商业联合会(Zhōnghuá Quánguó Gōngshāngyè Liánhéhuì):全国各类工商业者组成的人民团体,成立于 1953 年 10 月。

中华全国工商业联合会(the All-China Federation of Industry and Commerce) was founded in October 1953 by various industrialists and businessmen.

(三)报纸的"版(bǎn)"和"栏(lán)"

版(page) and **栏**(column) of a Newspaper

报纸的一面叫"一版"。中国的《人民日报》从周一到周五每天

12版,周六8版,周日4版。其他报纸从4版到12版不等。版名在各版外侧上角标明。

A page of a newspaper is known as 一版. The *People's Daily* has 12 pages every day from Monday to Friday, 8 pages on Saturday and 4 pages on Sunday. Other papers produce pages variously from 4 to 12. The page names are shown in the top corner of each page.

《人民日报》设有34个专版,版面大体上是这样安排的:

一、四版为"要闻",二版为"经济",三版为"政治·法律·社会",五版为"教育·科技·文化",六、七版为"国际",八版为"体育",九版为"理论"以及"读者来信"和"读者之友",十版为文学艺术方面的专版,十一版为"学术动态"以及国内政治方面的专版,十二版是"副刊"和副刊类的版面。其他各版定期刊出。

The *People's Daily* has 34 special sections and the layout is generally like this: the 1st and 4th pages are devoted to 要闻 (Yàowén, Important News); the 2nd page 经济 (Jīngjì, Economy); the 3rd page 政治,法律,社会 (Zhèngzhì, Fǎlù, Shèhuì, Politics, Law and Society); the 5th page 教育,科技,文化 (Jiàoyù, Kējì, Wénhuà, Education, Science and Technology, Culture); the 6th and 7th pages would be 国际 (Guójì, International); the 8th page is for 体育 (Tǐyù, Sports); the 9th page carries 理论 (Lǐlùn, Theory), 读者来信 (Dúzhě Láixìn, Letters to the Editor) and 读者之友 (Dúzhě Zhī Yǒu, Friend of Readers); the 10th page is taken up by literature and art section; the 11th page contains a special section for 学术动态 (Xuéshù Dòngtài, Development in Learning) and national politics; and the 12th pages is given to 副刊 (Fùkān, Supplement) and the kind. Other pages appear periodically.

除了"版"以外,还有"栏"。同一"栏"内刊载内容相近的新闻稿,用线条与其他新闻分隔,并有醒目的栏目名称。各报都有自己常设的或在某一时期为某一问题开设的栏目。《人民日报》的"社论"常被看作中国共产党和中国政府的指导性意见，受到人们的重视。

    Columns present news items of one type or another separated from other news stories with lines, bold titles. Each newspaper has its regular columns or special columns devoted to the focal issue for a certain period of time. The editorials of the *People's Daily* are often regarded as the guiding views expressed by the Chinese Communist Party.

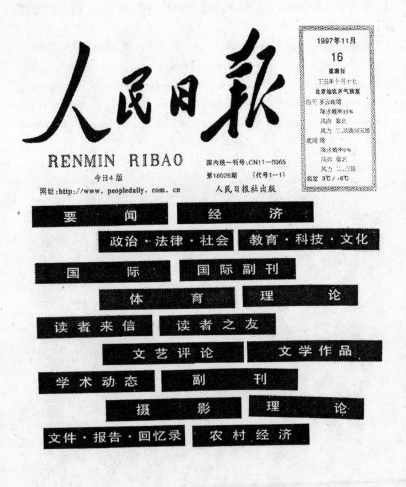

《人民日报》版面名称示例
Samples of page names in the *People's Daily*

《人民日报》版面栏目示例
Samples of Columns in the *People's Daily*

第三课 政 治
III. POLITICS

一、词语和句子

（一）关于领导和指导思想

1：以……为代表/核心/领导

---

(1) 为寻找一条在中国建设社会主义的正确道路，以毛泽东（Máo Zédōng）、周恩来（Zhōu Ēnlái）、刘少奇（Liú Shàoqí）、朱德（Zhū Dé）、邓小平（Dèng Xiǎopíng）、陈云（Chén Yún）等同志为代表的中国共产党人，已经探索多年。以江泽民（Jiāng Zémín）同志为核心的第三代领导人继续在探索中前进。（1991.4.12）

(2) 要继续坚持以经济建设为中心，下大力气提高经济效益。（1991.4.10）

2：在……领导/指引下

---

(1) 中共十三届三中全会以来，我国人民在中国共产党的

32

领导下,以经济建设为中心,坚持四项基本原则,坚持改革开放,开创了建设有中国特色的社会主义道路,社会主义现代化建设取得了巨大成就。(1991.1.3)

(2) 中国共产党十一届三中全会以来,全国人民在党的"一个中心,两个基本点"的基本路线指引下,胜利地实现了我国社会主义现代化建设的第一步战略目标。(1991.4.30)

(3) 在"一国两制"的方针指引下,有广大香港同胞的积极参与,香港的平稳过渡和长期繁荣稳定一定会实现。(1996.9.29)

(二) 关于目标和任务

1：目标/根本任务是……
---

(1) 今后十年的目标,是努力使全国人民的生活达到小康水平。(1991.4.11)

(2) 社会主义精神文明建设的根本任务,是培养有理想、有道德、有文化、有纪律的社会主义公民,提高整个中华民族的思想道德素质和科学文化水平。(1991.4.11)

2：……是……关键/保证/重要内容/首要问题
---

(1) 加强和改善中国共产党的领导,是社会主义事业不断

33

前进、保证十年规划和"八五"计划顺利实现的关键。(1991.4.15)

(2) 国家的统一,民族的团结,是我们各项事业取得成就的重要保证。(1996.9.12)

(3) 1987 年,中共十三大又明确提出共产党领导下的多党合作和政治协商制度是我国一项基本政治制度,并把坚持和完善这一制度作为政治体制改革的一项重要内容。(1991.6.14.光明)

(4) 密切各族人民的关系,加强各族人民的团结,认真贯彻党的民族政策,给终是西藏必须非常重视的首要问题。(1991.5.23)

(三) 生 词

1. 以…为…	yǐ…wéi…	to regard...as, to take...as
2. 核心	héxīn	nucleus, core
3. 寻找	xúnzhǎo	to seek, to look for
4. 探索	tànsuǒ	to explore, to probe
5. 代	dài	generation
6. 坚持	jiānchí	to persist in, to adhere to
7. 气力	qìlì	effort, strength
8. 效益	xiàoyì	benefit
9. 在…下	zài…xià	under
10. 指引	zhǐyǐn	guide
11. 开创	kāichuàng	to initiate, to pioneer, to create
12. 成就	chéngjiù	achievement
13. 路线	lùxiàn	line

14. 战略	zhànlüè	strategy
15. 参与	cānyù	to participate in
16. 过渡	guòdù	transition
17. 稳定	wěndìng	stable, steady
18. 小康	xiǎokāng	well-to-do; relatively comfortable (life)
19. 培养	péiyǎng	to train, to develop
20. 纪律	jìlǜ	discipline
21. 素质	sùzhì	quality, constitution
22. 关键	guānjiàn	key, crux
23. 首要	shǒuyào	of the first importance
24. 加强	jiāqiáng	to strengthen, to reinforce
25. 不断	bùduàn	unceasing, constant
26. 顺利	shùnlì	smooth, successful
27. 多党	duōdǎng	multi-party
28. 合作	hézuò	cooperation
29. 完善	wánshàn	to perfect, to improve
30. 密切	mìqiè	to build close links (between two parties)
31. 始终	shǐzhōng	from beginning to end; throughout

（四）专有名词

1. 香港	Xiānggǎng	Hong Kong
2. 中华民族	Zhōnghuá Mínzú	the Chinese nation

3. 西藏　　Xīzàng　　Xizang (Tibet) Autonomous region (in Southwest China)

二、阅读短文

（一）

乔石接受美国记者采访（节录）

问：全国人大与中国共产党的关系是怎样的？

答：中国共产党是社会主义事业的领导核心。国家机关在党的领导下工作。全国人大及其常委会在党的领导下，依法行使职权（zhíquán, powers of office）开展工作，努力贯彻党的路线、方针、政策，全心全意地为全国人民服务。党领导国家机关，但并不代替国家机关的工作。党的领导主要是政治、思想和组织的领导。党对国家事务的领导，主要是政治原则、政治方向、重大决策（juécè, policy decision）的领导和向国家机关推荐（tuījiàn, to recommend）重要干部。党组织关于国家事务的重大决策，凡是应当由人大和人大常委会决定的事项，都要经人大或人大常委会通过法定程序变成国家意志。（1996.12.15）

（二）

司马义·艾买提接见少数民族参观团时说

中华民族具有非常强的凝聚力

本报北京 9 月 29 日讯　［国家民委主任］司马义·艾买提（Sīmǎyì Àimǎití, Ismail Amat）今天在接见最近抵京的全国自治州少数民族参观团时说，中国在二千多年前即形成了统一的多民族国家的格局。各民族互相依存、共同发展，形成了谁也离不开谁的关系。中华民族具有非常强的凝聚力（níngjùlì, cohesion）和向心力（xiàngxīnlì, centripetal force）。

他说，社会主义事业和改革使得各民族获得了发展进步，给各民族人民带来了实惠（shíhuì, material benefit）……经济的发展和稳定，是社会稳定的基础，是人心稳定和各民族团结的重要条件。正反两方面的经验使各民族深深懂得必须珍视（zhēnshì, to cherish）民族大团结，必须捍卫（hànwèi, to defend）祖国的大统一。（1991.9.30）

三、练　习

（一）熟读下列词语：

(1) 国家统一　民族团结　一国两制
(2) 社会主义方向　社会主义道路　社会主义制度
　　社会主义事业　社会主义建设　社会主义初级阶段
(3) 现代化建设　精神文明建设　物质文明建设
(4) 以经济建设为中心,坚持四项基本原则,坚持改革开放。
(5) 坚持党的领导　坚持社会主义　坚持以经济建设为中心
　　坚持把思想工作放在首位

(二)请把下列短文译成外语:

在全国政协新年茶话会上江泽民同志的讲话(节录)

　　中国共产党领导的多党合作和政治协商制度,是我国的基本政治制度。人民政协是我国广泛的爱国统一战线组织,是发扬社会主义民主的重要渠道(qúdào, channel)。中国共产党将继续按照"长期共存,肝胆相照,荣辱与共"的方针,加强同各民主党派和无党派爱国人士的亲密合作。我们诚恳(chéngkěn, sincere)地希望人民政协积极履行(lǚxíng, to perform)政治协商、民主监督的职能(zhínéng, function)。(1992.1.2)

四、小　知　识
BACKGROUND INFORMATION

(一)中国共产党十一届三中全会 The Third Plenary Session of the Eleventh Central Committee of CPC

　　中国共产党第十一届中央委员会第三次全体会议于 1978 年 12 月 18 日至 22 日在北京举行。会议全面纠正了"文化大革命"的错误,重新确立了中国共产党的马克思主义路线,并决定把工作重点转移到社会主义现代化建设上来。这是中国当代政治生活中一次极为重要的会议。

The Third Plenary Session of the Eleventh Central Committee of CPC was held in Beijing between the 18th and 22nd December 1978. Decisions were made to thoroughly correct all mistakes resulted from ″the Cultural Revolution″, to re-establish the Marxist line as the CPC political line, and to shift the emphasis of work toward a drive for socialist modernization. It was a very important meeting in the political life of modern China.

（二）"一个中心，两个基本点"和"四项基本原则" ″One Centre and Two Basic Points″ and ″Four Cardinal Principles″

一个中心，两个基本点，即以经济建设为中心，坚持四项基本原则，坚持改革开放。这是中国共产党在现阶段的基本路线。

″One Centre and Two Basic Points″ means making economic development the central task, and adhering to the four cardinal principles and persisting in reform and opening up to the outside world, which is the CPC's basic line for the present stage.

四项基本原则是，必须坚持社会主义道路，必须坚持无产阶级专政，必须坚持共产党的领导，必须坚持马列主义、毛泽东思想。

″Four Cardinal Principles″ means resolute adherence to the socialist road, dictatorship of the proletariat, leadership by the Chinese Communist Party, and adherence to Marxism-Leninism and Mao Zedong Thought.

（三）中国实现和平统一的方针："一国两制" China's Policy for Realization of Peaceful Unification: ″One Country, Two Systems″

"一国两制"即一个国家，两种制度，是邓小平从中国的实际出发，实现和平统一的构想。其基本内容是：在一个中国的前提下，国家的主体坚持社会主义制度；香港、澳门、台湾是中华人民共和国不可分离的部分，它们作为特别行政区保持原有的资本主义制度长期不变。在国际上代表中国的，只能是中华人民共和国。

″One country, two systems″ is a concept of Deng Xiaoping for the realization of the peaceful unification according to China's actual condition. Its basic idea is: one China is the prerequisite, and the main body of China will keep socialist system; Hong Kong, Macao, Taiwan are an integral part of the People's Republic of China, and as special administrative regions will retain their capitalist system unchanged for a long time. In the international arena, only the People's Republic of China can represent China.

(四)中国社会主义现代化建设的战略目标 The Strategic Goal of the Drive for the Chinese Socialist Modernization

中国社会主义现代化建设的战略目标是从新中国成立时算起大约用 100 年左右的时间实现国家的现代化,第一步用 10 年时间,使 80 年代末国民生产总值比 1980 年翻一番,解决人民的温饱问题;第二步再用 10 年时间,到本世纪末,实现国民生产总值再翻一番,人民生活达到小康水平;第三步,到下世纪中叶,使人均国民生产总值达到中等发达国家水平,基本上实现国家的现代化。

China's modernization is to be fulfilled in 100 years beginning from the founding of New China in 1949. The first step is to provide enough food and better clothes for the people by increasing 1989's gross national product (GNP) to twice as much as that of 1980 in ten years time. The second step is to enable the Chinese people to become comparatively well-off by redoubling the GNP in another ten years. The third step is to fulfill the modernization by raising the GNP to the level of an average developed country by the middle of the next century.

第四课　统　计
IV. STATISTICS

一、词语和句子

（一）关于百分比

为/达……，占……

---

(1) 目前，天津市 6 岁以上具有各种文化程度的人口为
　　699.2317 万人，占总人口的 79.59％。(1991.4.3)
(2) 我国少数民族人口达 1 亿多，占全国总人口的
　　8.98％，民族地区面积占全国总面积的 64％。(1996.
　　9.6)

（二）关于增加

1：达到……，比……增长……　　增[长]/幅[度]
　翻一番

---

(1) 当月出口总值 141 亿美元，比上年同月增长 12.8％，

41

增幅比上月提高 11.5 个百分点。(1996.9.18)

(2) 中医药学是我国传统文化的重要组成部分。据不完全统计,1988 年以后,来华学习中医药的留学生人数达 14700 人次,是 1988 年以前来华学习中医药的留学生总人数的 36 倍。(1996.12.13)

(3) 太行山区阳谷庄乡以 98 万元的投入,获得了 3330 万元的经济效益,三年迈出三步,产值翻了两番。(1996.9.6)

2:增加到……　　上……台阶

---

(1) 1995 年,这个矿务局上缴的利税从 1985 年的 3337 万元增加到 8340 万元,为国家作出了重大贡献。(1996.11.11)

(2) 全球水产品总产量 1950 年只有 2000 万吨,到 60 年代就迈上了 5000 万吨的台阶,目前达到了 1 亿吨的水平。(1996.9.6)

(三) 关于减少

1:比……下降……　　　与……相比,下降……

---

(1) 由于部分旅客转向汽车和飞机,今年 1—6 月份,全国铁路客运量为 4.48 亿人次,比去年同期下降 14%。

（1996.11.8）

（2）值得注意的是：与去年同期相比，彩电的进口量下降了46.5％。（1996.9.12）

2：从/由……下降/减少/降低到……　回落……

（1）文盲占总人口的比例由建国初的80％下降到1995年的12.1％，青壮年中的文盲率已降到7％以下；全国8个省、直辖市、118个县（市、区）基本扫除了青壮年文盲。（1996.9.11）

（2）从1978年到1995年，全国农村贫困人口从2.5亿人减少到6500万人，由占世界贫困人口的1/4降低到1/20，这是一个巨大的历史成就。（1996.9.24）

（3）8月份，国有企业[完成增加值]比上年同月增长3.1％，比7月份增长速度回落1.5个百分点。（1996.9.10）

（三）生　词

1. 总	zǒng	total
2. 增长	zēngzhǎng	to increase
3. 幅[度]	fú[dù]	range, scope
增幅	zēngfú	scope of increase
4. 翻……番	fān...fān	to multiply by (a specified number of times)

5. 出口	chūkǒu	export
6. 值	zhí	value
总值	zǒngzhí	total value
7. 美元	měiyuán	US dollar
8. 百分点	bǎifēndiǎn	percentage point
9. 中医药学	zhōngyīyàoxué	traditional Chinese medical science
10. 据	jù	according to
11. 投入	tóurù	input
12. 迈	mài	to step
13. 产值	chǎnzhí	output value
14. 台阶	táijiē	step，stage
15. 矿务局	kuàngwùjú	mining bureau
16. 上缴	shàngjiǎo	to turn over
17. 利税	lìshuì	profits tax
18. 水产	shuǐchǎn	aquatic products
19. 产量	chǎnliàng	output，yield
20. 吨	dūn	tonne
21. 下降	xiàjiàng	to decrease
22. 相比	xiāngbǐ	to compare
23. 客运量	kèyùnliàng	passenger transport volume
24. 人次	réncì	person-time
25. 彩电	cǎidiàn	colour television set
26. 进口	jìnkǒu	import
27. 回落	huíluò	to fall back
28. 文盲	wénmáng	illiterate，illiteracy
29. 青壮年	qīng-zhuàngnián	youth and prime of life

30. 率	lǜ	rate
31. 直辖市	zhíxiáshì	municipality directly under the central government
32. 扫除	sǎochú	to eliminate，to wipe out
33. 贫困	pínkùn	impoverished
34. 国有	guóyǒu	state-owned
35. 企业	qǐyè	enterprise

（四）专有名词

1. 太行山	Ṭàihángshān	Taihang Mountain
2. 阳谷庄乡	Yánggǔzhuāng Xiāng	Yangguzhuang Township

二、阅读短文

（一）

北京人口已婚率（yǐhūnlǜ, the rate of the married）提高（节录）

北京人 15—19 岁、20—29 岁两个年龄段（niánlíngduàn，age group）的人口比例下降，分别比 5 年前下降了 1.77％和 5.76％，相反，50 岁以上人口比重则上升，增加 1.14％。

目前，有配偶（pèi'ǒu, spouse）人口占 75.33％，比 5 年前上升了 3.13％。但年轻人有配偶比例下降，年长者有配偶比例上升。调查中，北京人的离婚率（líhūnlǜ, the rate of the divorced）为 1％，比 5 年前上升 0.27％。从年龄段看，50 岁以下的中青年离婚率迅速上升，而 50 岁以上人口离婚率呈下降趋势，比 5 年前下降了 0.04％。离婚率最高的年龄段为 30—39 岁，而 5 年前是 40—49 岁，离婚人口正年轻化。（《北京日报》，1996.11.9）

46

（二）

水产品是优质粮食

　　全球（quánqiú，the whole world）水产品总产量 1950 年只有 2000 万吨，到 60 年代就迈上了 5000 万吨的台阶，目前达到了 1 亿吨的水平。一个最基本的原因，就是人类对水产品需求量的增加。据有关资料介绍，日本和我国台湾省每年人均直接消费粮食都只有 90 公斤，但人均消费水产品却很高，日本高达 80 公斤。

　　我国建国初期的短短几年中，水产量就从 1949 年 40 多万吨增长到 1957 年的 312 万吨。1985 年以来，我国渔业进入了快速发展的新时期，1990 年起水产品产量跃居（yuè jū，leap to）世界首位，去年，达到了 2517 万吨，占全球总产量的 1/4，年均增长率高达 11.6％，而同期世界的平均增长率只有 2—3％。（1996.9.6）

（三）

我国钢产量跃居世界第一
年产量突破一亿吨　产销率保持在99％左右

　　【本报北京12月31日电】　冶金部部长刘淇（Liú Qí）今天宣布：1996年我国钢产量突破1亿吨，跃居世界第一位。这是我国钢铁工业发展进程中一个新的里程碑。

　　据介绍，我国从1890年张之洞（Zhāng Zhīdòng）创办汉阳铁厂到1948年的半个多世纪中，产钢总量仅760万吨。新中国成立后八年，全国钢产量达到535万吨。从1978年到"六五"末期，钢产量从3178万吨提高到4679万吨。从80年代末到90年代，我国钢铁工业发展进一步加快：1989年钢产量超过6000万吨，1991年超过7000万吨，1992年超过8000万吨，1994年超过9000万吨。更为可喜的是，在数量快速增长的同时，我国钢铁工业结构也发生了巨大的变化。工艺技术落后的平炉钢（pínglúgāng，open-hearth steel）的比重，1996年仅为12％，比建国初期下降了67个百分点。转炉钢（zhuànlúgāng，converter steel）1996年占70％，比建国初期上升了69个百分点。……目前，我国钢材自给率已达到88％，产销率保持在99％左右。（1997.1.1）

汉阳铁厂　Hànyáng Tiěchǎng　the Hanyang Iron Plant

三、练　习

(一)请把下列数字按句型组成句子:

"____产量 1990 年达到(为)____,比上年增长(减少)____%"

	1990 年	比上年(%)
粮食总产量	43500 万吨	6.7%
棉花产量	477 万吨	18.1%
布产量	180 亿米	-4.9%
电视机产量	2667 万部	-3.8%　(1991.2.23)

(二)把下列句子译成外语:

(1) 全公司销售(xiāoshòu, sale)收入由 1984 年的 1920 万元,增长到 1995 年的 4.5 亿元,[增长]了 22 倍多。(1996.11.28)

(2) 油料全年播种(bōzhòng, sown)面积比去年减少 825 万亩,[下降]4.2%。(1996.11.29)

(3) 据民政部统计,1995 年,我国离婚对数已达 104.5 万对,突破百万大关,[比]上年的 97.1 万对[增加]了 7.4 万对,是同年结婚人数的 11.3%。据报载,北京市的离婚人数[占]当年结婚人数的 25%。(1996.9.6)

(4) 今年前三个季度(jìdù, quarter of a year)香港旅游收入达 610 亿元,比去年[同期]上升 16.5%,再创新记录。(1996.11.27)

四、小　知　识
BACKGROUND INFORMATION

(一)中国的五年计划 China's Five-Year Plans

中国政府为了有计划地进行经济建设,从 1953 年,实施国民经济和社会发展五年计划。历次五年计划的时间是:

In order to carry out the economic construction in a planned way, the Chinese Government began the first Five-Year Plan for National Economy and Social Development in 1953. The following are the starting and ending years of the successive Five-Year Plans:

1. 1953~1957　　2. 1958~1962
3. 1966~1970　　4. 1971~1975
5. 1976~1980　　6. 1981~1985
7. 1986~1990　　8. 1991~1995
9. 1996~2000

实施第 X 个五年计划的时间就叫"X 五期间"。

The years for the "Xth" Five-Year Plan is known as "X 五期间".

(二)若干常见的中国共产党和中国政府机关的简称 Some Useful Abbreviations for the Organizations of the Chinese Communist Party and Government

除了第 I、II 专题里提到的若干简称外,常见的中国党和政府机关的简称还有:

Apart from the abbreviations appearing in the first and second chapters there are some more useful abbreviations for the organizations of the Chinese Communist Party and government:

1. 党中央——中国共产党中央委员会

党中央 for 中国共产党中央委员会（the Central
Committee of the Communist Party of China）

中委——中央委员会,中央委员

中委 for 中央委员会,中央委员（the Central Committee,
the member of the Central Committee）

中央军委——中国共产党中央军事委员会

中央军委 for 中国共产党中央军事委员会（the Military
Commission of the CPC Central Committee）

中办——中央委员会办公厅

中办 for 中央委员会办公厅（the General Office of the
Central Committee）

中组部——中央委员会组织部

中组部 for 中央委员会组织部（the Organization
Department of the Central Committee）

中宣部——中央委员会宣传部

中宣部 for 中央委员会宣传部（the Publicity Department
of the Central Committee）

中联部——中央委员会对外联络部

中联部 for 中央委员会对外联络部（the Liaison
Department of the Central Committee）

中直机关——中央委员会直属机关

中直机关 for 中央委员会直属机关（the Institutions
Directly under the Central Committee）

党委——中国共产党委员会

党委 for 中国共产党委员会（the Committee of the
Communist Party of China）

省/市/县委——中国共产党 省/市/县 委员会

省/市/县委 for 中国共产党 省/市/县 委员会（the
Provincial/Municipal/County Committee of the Communist
Party of China）

2. 国办——国务院办公厅

国办 for 国务院办公厅 (the General Office of the State Council)

国家计委——国家计划委员会

国家计委 for 国家计划委员会 (the State Planning Commission)

国家教委——国家教育委员会

国家教委 for 国家教育委员会 (the Ministry of Education)

国家语委——国家语言文字工作委员会

国家语委 for 国家语言文字工作委员会 (the State Language Work Committee)

计生委——计划生育委员会

计生委 for 计划生育委员会 (Family Planning Commission)

外经贸部——对外贸易经济合作部

外经贸部 for 对外贸易经济合作部 (the Ministry of Foreign Trade and Economic Cooperation)

民航局——中国民用航空管理局

民航局 for 中国民用航空管理局 (Civil Aviation Administration of China)

国务院各个部和委员会合称国务院各部委

国务院各部委 is short for 国务院各个部和委员会 (Ministries and Commissions of the State Council)

3. 总政——中国人民解放军总政治部

总政 for 中国人民解放军总政治部 (the General Political Department of the Chinese People's Liberation Army)

总参——中国人民解放军总参谋部

总参 for 中国人民解放军总参谋部 (the Headquarters of the General Staff of the Chinese People's Liberation Army)

总后——中国人民解放军总后勤部

总后 for 中国人民解放军总后勤部（the General Logistics Department of the Chinese People's Liberation Army）

总政、总参、总后合称解放军三总部

解放军三总部（PLA Three General Departments）is short for 总政，总参 and 总后.

中国人民解放军的各个军种和兵种合称解放军各军兵种

解放军各军兵种 is short for 中国人民解放军的各个军种和兵种（PLA Arms and Services）.

4. 中国共产党、中国政府、中国人民解放军和群众团体合称党政军群

党政军群 is short for 中国共产党，中国政府，中国人民解放军 and 群众团体（the Communist Party of China，the Chinese Government，the Chinese People's Liberation Army and mass organizations）.

第五课 经　济
V. ECONOMY

一、词语和句子

（一）关于国民经济指标

> 1：国民生产总值　国内生产总值　可比价格

（1）实行改革开放的十八年以来，中国的国民生产总值保持了年均 9% 以上的增长速度。（1996.9.20）

（2）1995 年国内生产总值达 57277.3 亿元，按可比价格计算，提前 5 年实现了翻两番的目标。（1996.11.15）

> 2：总产量　总产值

（1）中国依靠自己的力量，解决了人民的吃饭问题。1995 年中国粮食总产量达到 4.66 亿多吨，比 1949 年增长 3 倍，远远高于同期人口的增长幅度。（1996.11.16）

（2）今年天津开发区已实现国内生产总值 93.6 亿元、工业总产值 331 亿元、利润 37.5 亿元、出口额 9.8 亿

元。(1996.10.24)

3：价格总水平　人均（纯）收入　人均支出
　　生活消费

---

(1) 10 月份全国商品零售价格总水平比去年同期上升
　　4.7％,比今年 9 月份下降 0.3％。(1996.11.12)
(2) 据统计,1995 年辽宁省农村居民家庭人均纯收入为
　　1756.5 元,高于全国平均水平,今年预计为 2050 元。
　　1—9 月份农民人均生活消费支出为 897.32 元,比去
　　年同期增长 29.5％。(1996.11.24)

4：国际收支　出（进）口货物总额　入（出）超

国际收支显著改善:去年出口货物总额为六百二十
亿六千万美元,进口五百三十三亿五千万美元,出大
于进,扭转了一九八四年以来连年入超状况。(1991.
2.22)

（二）关于经济发展

1：发展模式　国情
　　经济体制　社会主义市场经济

---

(1) 各国情况不尽相同,不可能有统一的发展模式,各国都要根据自己的国情决定自己的发展道路。(1991. 4.13)

(2) 当前的中国正在大力推进现代化进程,实现建立和完善社会主义市场经济体制的目标,到下世纪中叶赶上或超过中等发达国家的水平。(1996.11.14)

2:公有制　国有经济　国有资产　国有企业　个体经济　私营经济

---

(1) 改革开放以来,中国在坚持社会主义公有制为主体的前提下,允许个体经济、私营经济和其他经济成分的发展,这也是我国经济改革的一项重要措施。(1991. 6.8)

(2) 国有企业改革是中国经济体制改革的中心环节。几年来,我们对市场经济条件下国有经济的有关问题进行了重大而艰难的探索。(1996.11.15)

(三) 生　词

1. 国民生产总值　guómín shēngchǎn zǒngzhí　gross national product (GNP)

2. 国内生产总值　guónèi shēngchǎn zǒngzhí　gross domestic product (GDP)

3. 可比价格　kěbǐ jiàgé　comparable price

	价格	jiàgé	price
4.	依靠	yīkào	to rely on，to depend on
5.	粮食	liángshi	grain，food
6.	开发区	kāifāqū	development zone
	开发	kāifā	development；to develop
7.	…额	é	volume or amount
8.	人均	rénjūn	per capita
9.	零售	língshòu	retail
10.	上升	shàngshēng	to go up，to rise
11.	居民	jūmín	resident，inhabitant
12.	纯	chún	net
13.	预计	yùjì	to estimate
14.	货物	huòwù	goods
15.	入超	rùchāo	to excess of imports over exports
16.	扭转	niǔzhuǎn	to turn back，to reverse
17.	模式	móshì	pattern
18.	国情	guóqíng	national conditions
19.	体制	tǐzhì	system
20.	市场经济	shìchǎng jīngjì	market economy
21.	推进	tuījìn	to push forward
22.	进程	jìnchéng	course，process
23.	中叶	zhōngyè	middle period
24.	超过	chāoguò	to surpass
25.	发达国家	fādá guójiā	developed country
26.	公有制	gōngyǒuzhì	public ownership (of means of production)

27. 国有经济 guóyǒu jīngjì　　　national economy
28. 个体经济 gètǐ jīngjì　　　　individual economy
29. 私营经济 sīyíng jīngjì　　　the private sector of
　　　　　　　　　　　　　　economy
30. 措施　　cuòshī　　　　　　measure，step
31. 面向　　miànxiàng　　　　to cater to，to be
　　　　　　　　　　　　　　geared to
32. 环节　　huánjié　　　　　　link，sector

（四）专有名词

辽宁省　Liáoníng Shěng　a province in Northeast China

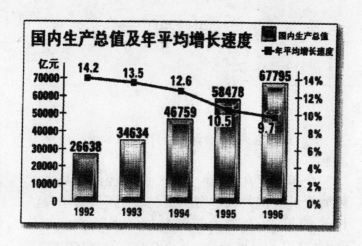

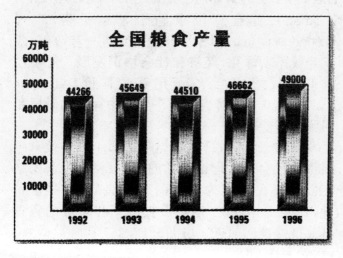

《人民日报》1997.9.27）

59

二、阅读短文

（一）《人民日报》社论：

把握大局，继续前进（节录）

今年，是"九五"第一年。整个经济形势继续朝着好的方向发展。显著标志是：既保持了经济快速增长，又有效地抑制（yìzhì，to restrain，to check）了通货膨胀（tōnghuò péngzhàng，inflation）；社会总供求趋于基本平衡，宏观（hóngguān，macro）经济环境得到进一步改善；改革开放不断深化，经济和社会协调发展。对于已取得的成绩，应当给予足够的估价（gūjià，to evaluate）。同时，对当前经济生活中存在的矛盾和问题也不能低估。

新的一年里，只要我们坚持邓小平建设有中国特色社会主义理论和党的基本路线，紧密团结在以江泽民同志为核心的党中央周围，振奋精神，扎实工作，就一定能够把改革和发展的各项事业继续推向前进。（1996.12.25）

(二)

当前,我国社会安定,国民经济持续、快速、健康发展,围绕建立社会主义市场经济体制的各项改革取得新的进展。我国同各国在经济、贸易、科技、文化等领域的合作交流进一步扩大。我国的综合国力显著增强。在进行经济建设的同时,我们也重视社会主义精神文明建设,为我国经济和社会的健康发展提供有力的支持和保证。(1996.9.29)

三、练　习

(一)熟读下列词语:
(1) 国民经济　国民生产　国民收入
(2) 国民生产总值　国内生产总值　工业生产总值
　　农业生产总值　国民收入总值
(3) 工业总产量　农业总产量　粮食总产量
(4) 经济体制　社会主义市场经济　计划经济
　　经济成分　国有经济　集体经济　私营经济　个体经济
(5) 运行机制　价格机制

(二)请把下列短文译成外语:
今年年初,中国制定了第九个五年计划和 2010 年远景(yuǎnjǐng, prospect)目标。按照这个发展规划,到 2000 年,在全国人口比 1980 年增加 3 亿左右的情况下,将实现人均国民生产总值比 1980 年翻两番,人民生活达到小康(xiǎokāng, relatively

comfortable 〈life〉)水平,并初步建立社会主义市场经济体制。到 2010 年,将实现国民生产总值比 2000 年再翻一番。实现了上述目标,中国的综合(zōnghé,comprehensive)国力和人民生活水平都将再上一个大台阶,为下个世纪中叶基本实现现代化奠定(diàndìng,to establish)坚实的基础。(1996.9.5)

四、小　知　识
BACKGROUND INFORMATION

(一)关于国民经济几个指标的概念 The Definition of Some Chinese Terms of National Economy

○工农业总产值:它反映一年内生产的工农业产品的全部价值。在计算上,以各种产品产量乘上其价格,然后相加,所得结果就是工农业总产值。由于采用"工厂法"计算,厂与厂之间协作越多,重复计算的次数也越多,夸大了全社会实际的生产规模和水平。

工农业总产值(the total value of industrial and agricultural output):It shows the total value of the industrial and agricultural products produced in one year. The statistics are worked out by adding the numbers taken from multiplying the quantity of all products by their prices. The "factory calculation" may lead to the overestimation of the size and level of the actual social production as a whole, because more coordinations between different factories would mean more repeated calculations.

○社会总产值:它是农业、工业、建筑业、运输邮电业和商业饮食业五个物质生产部门总产值之和,也包括了重复计算在内。

社会总产值(the gross value of social output):It is the total output value of agriculture, industry, construction, transportation, post and telecommunication, commerce and catering trade. The result includes overlapping calculation.

○国民收入:指国民收入生产额,也包括上述五大经济部门。在价值计算上,只计算劳动者新创造的价值,也就是说,没有重复计算。

国民收入(national income):It indicates the total value produced by different sectors of national economy, including the above-said five ones. The statistics are worked out by only calculating the value that the working people have brought about. In other words, the overlapping calculation is thus avoided.

○国民生产总值:它是一个国家(或地区)在一定时期所生产的最终产品和提供的劳务总量的货币表现。它包括上述五大物质生产部门和服务业、公用事业、金融保险业、科研文教卫生事业、国家机关、国防等非物质生产部门。在计算上,只计算新增加的价值,没有重复计算。

国民生产总值(gross national product):It is a monetary expression of the final products made in a certain period of time and the total amount of labour provided by a country (or a region). It involves the above-said five sectors of material production, as well as the sectors of non-material production such as the service trade, public utilities, finance and insurance, scientific research, cultural, educational and health work, government offices and national defence. The statistics are worked out by only calculating the value that has been added without any repetition.

由于中国在生产过程中物质消耗比较高,因此,工农业总产值和社会总产值包括的增加值还比较低,有时会出现工农业总产值或社会总产值大于国民生产总值的情况。(据1991.4.26《人民日报》)

Due to the greater consumption of materials in the process of production in China, the value added to the total value of industrial and agricultural output and the gross value of social output is comparatively low. Sometimes the total value of industrial and agricultural output, or the gross value of social output can be greater than the gross national product.

(taken from the *People's Daily*, 26. 4. 1991)

○国内生产总值:是指按国土原则计算的一个国家或地区物质生产部门和非物质生产部门,在一定时期内所生产和提供最终使用的产品及劳务的货币表现。这些最终产品和劳务不论是本国还是外国居民投资、生产的,只要在这个国家的领土范围之内,就全部计算在内。(据《人民日报》1995.3.5)

国内生产总值 (gross domestic product): It is a monetary expression of the final products and labour made and provided by the material and non-material productive sectors of a country or region in a certain period of time. All the final products and labour, if invested and produced by domestic or foreign residents on the territory of this country, will be calculated.

(taken from the *People's Daily*, 5. 3. 1995)

(二)发达国家、发展中国家和最不发达国家 Developed Country, Developing Country and Most-Underdeveloped Country

这是为反映世界各国经济状况而使用的概念。

These terms are used to reflect the economic situation of every country in the world.

发达国家即高收入国家,是指人均国民生产总值高(世界银行1992年标准为高于1.2万美元)、工业化完成,教育、卫生和文化事业发达,基础设施良好的国家。包括西欧主要国家、美国、加拿大、日本和澳大利亚等国。

A developed country, i. e. high-income country, has high per capita gross national product (GNP) (the World Bank's standard in 1992 is above 12000 US dollars), completed industrialization, well-developed educational, health and cultural undertakings, and good infrastructure. Developed countries include major Western

European countries, United States, Canada, Japan and Australia.

发展中国家是指人均国民生产总值低(1992 年世界银行标准为低于 7510 美元),在发展初期阶段,或尚处于工业化过程中,教育、卫生、文化事业欠发达,基础设施不完备的国家。

A developing country has low per capita GNP (the World Bank's 1992 standard is below 7510 US dollars). It is in the primary phase of development or still in the process of industrialization, and has undeveloped educational, health and cultural undertakings and uncompleted infrastructure.

最不发达国家的人均国民生产总值低于 699 美元(1994 年);其他人均寿命、人均热量摄入量、自然条件、就业状况等都比较差。1994 年底联合国批准的最不发达国家共 48 个。其中非洲 33 国,亚洲 9 国,美洲 1 国,大洋洲 5 国。(据《人民日报》1995.12.10)

A most-underdeveloped country's per capita GNP is lower than 699 US dollars (1994); average life span, average per capita calorie volume, natural condition, employment condition, etc. are comparatively poor. By the end of 1994, 48 most-underdeveloped countries were approved by the United Nations. Among these countries there are 33 in Africa, 9 in Asia, 1 in America and 5 in Oceania.

(taken from the *People's Daily*, 10.12.1995)

第六课　工　　业
VI. INDUSTRY

一、词语和句子

（一）关于工业产品

> ……投产／问世　研制／开发／推出……

(1)（标题）天津开发区两企业建成投产(1996.11.1)
瑞琪(Ruìqí)净水器在北京问世(1996.9.11)
(2)（简讯）章光 101(Zhāngguāng 101)集团推出美容护肤新品　北京章光 101 集团日前又以我国中草药研制、开发出美容护肤新品。(1996.10.22)

（二）关于工业体制

> 国有企(工)业　集体所有制企(工)业　乡镇企(工)业
> 国有经济　非国有经济　　公有制经济　集体经济

(1) 要通过深化企业改革,加快转换企业经营机制,增强国有企业、集体所有制企业的市场竞争能力,保证公有制经济在国民经济中的主导地位,发挥国有经济在国民经济中的主导作用。(1996.11.28)

(2) 10月份国有工业增长有所加快,比上年同月增长8.3%,为今年以来增幅最高的一个月。非国有经济继续快速增长。集体经济增长16.6%,其他经济工业增长11.5%。(1996.11.8)

(3) 改革开放十多年来,我国乡镇企业得到持续、快速、健康发展。去年全国乡镇企业已达到2203万个。今年1—9月,全国乡镇工业累计完成工业增加值5380亿元,比上年同期增长24—55%。(1996.11.28)

（三）关于工业改革

1：经济效益　社会效益
　　经营机制　自主经营　自负盈亏
　　商品生产者　商品经营者

---

(1) 对社会主义企业,乃至对我们社会主义国家的一切企业都应该提出经济效益和社会效益统一的要求。(1991.1.17)

(2) 各级领导务必高度重视经济发展中存在的困难、问题和矛盾,要采取切实有效措施,以提高经济效益为中心,集中力量搞活企业。(1991.6.21.光明)

(3) 搞活企业的关键是转换经营机制,使企业真正成为自

主经营、自负盈亏的社会主义商品生产者和经营者。(1991.1.11)

(4) 通过加大企业联合、改组、兼并、破产的力度,国有资产的优化和重组取得了明显的效果。(1996.11.15)

2: 产品结构

搞活分配　计件工资　奖金挂钩　全额承包

---

(1) 企业内部经济责任制,是我国 10 多年改革中办好企业的一项基本的、富有成效的重要制度。(1991.7.12)

(2) 在嘉丰棉纺厂,调整产品结构的速度是惊人的,国际市场上什么产品卖价高、投入少、产出多,他们就翻改什么品种。(1991.5.14)

(3) 搞活职工分配,厂内实行计件工资、奖金挂钩、全额承包三种分配方式,有力地调动起职工积极性。(1991.1.22)

(四) 生　词

1. 投产	tóuchǎn	to put into production, to go in to operation
2. 问世	wènshì	to come out, to appear
3. 研制	yánzhì	to develop, to research and manufacture

4. 推出	tuīchū	to produce	
5. 净水器	jìngshuǐqì	water purifier	
6. 集团	jítuán	group	
7. 美容	měiróng	to improve (esp. a woman's) looks	
8. 护肤	hùfū	to nourish face	
9. 日前	rìqián	a few days ago	
10. 中草药	zhōngcǎoyào	Chinese herbal medicine	
11. 集体	jítǐ	collective	
12. 所有制	suǒyǒuzhì	ownership	
13. 乡镇	xiāngzhèn	villages and towns	
14. 深化	shēnhuà	to deepen	
15. 加快	jiākuài	to quicken, to speed up	
16. 转换	zhuǎnhuàn	to transform, to change	
17. 经营	jīngyíng	to manage, to operate	
18. 机制	jīzhì	mechanism	
19. 竞争	jìngzhēng	to compete; competition	
20. 主体	zhǔtǐ	main part	
21. 主导	zhǔdǎo	leading, dominant	
22. 累计	lěijì	to add up	
23. 自主	zìzhǔ	to act on one's own, to be independent	
24. 自负盈亏	zìfù yíngkuī	(of an enterprise) to assume sole responsibility for its profits and losses	
25. 改组	gǎizǔ	to reorganize	
26. 兼并	jiānbìng	to merge, to annex	

27. 破产　　pòchǎn　　　　to go bankrupt
28. 力度　　lìdù　　　　　 dynamic
29. 资产　　zīchǎn　　　　property，assets
30. 优化　　yōuhuà　　　　to optimize
31. 采取　　cǎiqǔ　　　　 to take or assume，to adopt
32. 搞活　　gǎohuó　　　　to enliven
33. 结构　　jiégòu　　　　structure
34. 计件工资 jìjiàn gōngzī　 piece rate wage
35. 奖金挂钩 jiǎngjīn guàgōu bonus linkup
36. 全额　　quán'é　　　　total amount
37. 富有成效 fùyǒu chéngxiào to achieve remarkable success

（五）专有名词

1. 章光 101 集团　Zhāngguāng 101 Jítuán
　　　　　　　　　　the Zhangguang 101 Group
2. 嘉丰棉纺厂　Jiāfēng Miánfǎngchǎng
　　　　　　　　　　the Jiafeng Cotton Mill

二、阅读短文

我国原油年产突破 1.5 亿吨
提前实现国家提出的 2000 年原油产量目标

据中国石油天然气总公司统计资料表明,截至 12 月 14 日,我国原油(yuányóu, crude oil)产量达到 1.5 亿吨。这是继 1978 年以来踏上的又一个大的台阶。

1965 年,由于大庆油田的开发,我国原油年产量达到 1000 万吨,实现原油的基本自给。1978 年产油达到 1 亿吨,使我国进入世界产油大国的行列。"七五"、"八五"期间,陆上石油工业在勘探(kāntàn, prospecting)开发难度越来越大的情况下,实施"稳定东部,开发西部"的战略,原油产量连年稳中有升,海洋石油开发也逐年上升,全国原油产量终于在今年突破(tūpò, to break, to top)1.5 亿吨大关。预计全年可超过 1.55 亿吨,提前实现国家提出的 2000 年原油产量的目标。
(1996.12.15)

1. 中国石油天然气总公司　Zhōngguó Shíyóu Tiānránqì Zǒnggōngsī　the Petroleum and Gas Company of China
2. 大庆油田　Dàqìng Yóutián　the Daqing Oilfield

三、练　习

(一)熟读下列词语：

(1) 新产品研制　新产品开发　新产品投产　新产品问世
研制新产品　开发新产品　推出新产品

(2) 国有企/工业　集体企/工业　乡镇企/工业

(3) 经济效益　社会效益

(4) 经营机制　价格机制　运行机制

(5) 计件工资　计时工资

(二)请把下列短文译成外语：

南京熊猫电子集团走向世界

南京无线电厂在改革开放的年代，转变观念，转换经营机制，实现了"三级跳"。一是跳出厂门：1980 年 7 月，同南京地区 37 家中小电子(diànzǐ, electronics)企业组建了我国电子工业第一个横向(héngxiàng, horizontal)经济联合体；二是跳出城门：1987 年 5 月，跨出南京，联合 20 多个省、市、自治区的 150 多个企事业单位成立了熊猫(Xióngmāo, panda)电子集团；三是跳出国门：1987 年在美国合资建立了 VSI 公司和熊猫电子美国有限公司，走出了"国际合作开发——国内生产——国际销售"的路子。(1996. 12. 3)

1. 南京无线电厂　Nánjīng Wúxiàndiàn Chǎng　the Nanjing Radio Factory

2. 熊猫电子美国有限公司　Xióngmāo Diànzǐ Měiguó Yǒuxiàn Gōngsī　the Panda Electronics US Co. Ltd.

四、小 知 识
BACKGROUND INFORMATION

(一)"三资"企业 Enterprises in the "Three Forms of Ventures"

这是简缩的说法,指中外合资经营企业、中外合作经营企业和外商独资经营企业。它们是外商在中国投资的三种不同的方式。

The abbreviation stands for Sino-foreign joint ventures, enterprises jointly managed by China and foreign countries and ventures solely with the investment of foreign capital. These are the three different ways the foreign businessmen can invest in China.

(二)企业内部经济责任制 System of Economic Responsibility Within an Enterprise

这是中国工厂内部管理上的一项重要改革。它的主要内容是把工厂的生产分解为若干方面(如产品质量、产量、经济效益、生产安全、技术改造等),并定出一定的指标;根据这些指标对每个职工的生产情况按月进行考核,由此决定他们各自的收入(工资和奖金)。各企业因为情况不同有不同的实施办法。这一制度打破了传统的平均主义分配办法,体现了按劳分配的原则,把企业的生产、经营情况跟职工的经济利益联系起来(也就是人们常说的"挂钩"),调动了职工的生产积极性,促进了生产的发展。

This is an important reform in the internal management of Chinese factories. By the system targets are set for the quality and quantity of the products, economic benefits, safety, technological transformations, by which every worker or staff member is monthly checked on, and the results determine their income (wages and premiums). The management may vary from one enterprise to another in line with different conditions, but it has broken through the traditional equalitarianist method of distribution all the same. As a system of distribution according to work, it links the production and management with the economic benefits of the staff and workers (also known as " linkup"). Consequently their enthusiasm for production is aroused, and an advance in production is brought about.

(三)调整结构 Adjusting the Structure

指处理好工业与农业之间、轻工业与重工业之间、基础工业与加工工业之间、国防工业和民用工业之间以及第三产业与其他部门之间等方面的关系。

It means the proper handling of the relations between industry and agriculture, light industry and heavy industry, fundamental industry and processing industry, national defense industry and civilian industry, the tertiary industry and other sectors.

(四)计件工资和计时工资 Piece Rate Wages and Time Rate Wages

计件工资是按工人完成合格产品数量来计算其工资报酬的一种工资形式。计时工资是按工人的工作时间和熟练程度来计算工资的一种工资形式。

"Piece rate wages" is a wage system by which workers are paid in accordance with the quantity of the products that he has made to fixed standards. "Time rate wages" is another payment system by which workers are paid for the working hours and skills he uses.

第七课 农 业
VII. AGRICULTURE

一、词语和句子

（一）关于农业生产

粮食　　皮棉　　油料　　水产品

(1) 粮食在去年较大幅度增产的基础上，再创历史最高水平，预计总产量可超过 4800 亿公斤，比上年增产 135 万公斤以上。(1996.12.20)

(2) "丰收计划"实施 10 年来，共完成农牧渔业技术推广项目 257 项，累计增产粮食 300 亿公斤，皮棉 8 亿公斤，油料 37 亿公斤，肉蛋及水产品 14.6 亿公斤，新增产值 400 亿元。(1996.9.24)

（二）关于农业政策和农业发展

1：农业是国民经济的基础　　家庭联产承包责任制　　科教兴国/农

(1) 农业是国民经济的基础,无论什么时候都要把农业放到十分重要的位置。(1991.1.9)

(2) 解决 11 亿人口的吃饭问题是头等大事,是经济发展、社会安定、国家自立的基础。(1991.3.2)

(3) 以家庭联产承包为主的责任制是党在农村的基本政策,应在稳定的前提下,逐步加以完善。(1991.1.19)

(4) 我们实施"科教兴国"的战略,科教兴农是一个重要方面。中国有很多中低产田,依靠技术提高粮食产量的潜力很大。(1996.9.29)

2:乡镇企业　乡村工业　以工补/养农

---

(1) 乡镇企业是国民经济的重要组成部分,是农村经济的主要支柱。这些年,乡镇企业发展速度很快。"八五"期间全国国内生产总值净增量的 30%,工业增加值净增量的 50%,……均来自乡镇企业。(1996.11.1)

(2) 无锡县农村向工业化转变过程中,不断用乡村工业实力"反哺"农业,"以工补农","以工养农",工农业稳步协调发展。(1991.3.5)

(三) 关于农村的变化

贫困人口　温饱　脱贫　扶贫

（1）辽宁省农民普遍解决了温饱问题,但农户间收入差异扩大,相当一部分农民比较富裕,一小部分农民尚未脱贫。大石桥市富裕、比较富裕、一般三种类型的农民占农民总人口的比例为 2:5:3。(1996.11.24)

（2）中央扶贫开发工作会议召开……到本世纪末基本解决贫困人口温饱问题,这是党中央、国务院既定的战略目标。(1996.9.24)

（四）生　词

1. 皮棉	pímián	ginned cotton
2. 丰收	fēngshōu	bumper harvest
3. 实施	shíshī	to put into effect, to implement
4. 牧业	mùyè	animal husbandry
5. 渔业	yúyè	fishery
6. 项目	xiàngmù	item
7. 联产	liánchǎn	to link to output
8. 承包	chéngbāo	to contract
9. 责任制	zérènzhì	responsibility system
10. 兴国/农	xīng guó/nóng	to rejuvenate a country /vigorously develop agriculture
11. 头等大事	tóuděng dàshì	a matter of primary importance
12. 自立	zìlì	to support oneself

13. 加以	jiāyǐ	(used before a disyllabic verb to indicate the action is directed towards sth. or sb. mentioned earlier in the sentence)
14. 中低产	zhōng-dīchǎn	middle-low yield
低产	dīchǎn	low yield
15. 潜力	qiánlì	potential
16. 补	bǔ	to nourish
17. 养	yǎng	to support
18. 支柱	zhīzhù	pillar
19. 净	jìng	net
20. 稳步	wěnbù	steadily
21. 反哺	fǎnbǔ	to feed in return
22. 协调	xiétiáo	coordinated，harmonious
23. 温饱	wēnbǎo	to have adequate food and clothing
24. 脱贫	tuōpín	to be lifted out of poverty
25. 扶贫	fúpín	to assist the poor
26. 类型	lèixíng	kind，type
27. 既定	jìdìng	set，fixed

（五）专有名词

1. 无锡县　Wúxī Xiàn（现改为锡山市 Xīshān Shì）　a county in Jiangsu Province（now renamed and changed to a city）

2. 大石桥市　Dàshíqiáo Shì　a city in Liaoning Province

二、阅读短文

（一）

发展农业要把科技放在首位

我国农业可以用两句话来概括（gàikuò，to generalize）：一句是建国以来特别是改革开放以来，我国农业有了很大发展，我国用占世界7％的耕地（gēngdì，cultivated land）养活了占世界22％的人口，这是了不起的成就；一句是：我国农业发展仍然滞后（zhìhòu，to lag behind），与国民经济和人民生活日益增长的需求，还不相适应，我国71.1％以上的人从事农业、种地搞饭吃，说明我国农业的集约化（jíyuēhuà，to intensify）、现代化水平还很低。

发展农业的希望在科技，潜力在科技，出路在科技，发展农业要把科技放在首位。（1996.5.31）

(二)

"华夏第一县"实施文化建设十大工程

连续 3 年排行(páiháng, to rank)"中国农村综合实力百强县(市)"之首、有"华夏第一县"之称的江苏省锡山市,一手抓经济建设,一手抓精神文明建设,使经济和各项社会事业同步发展,被命名为"全国文化工作先进地区"。为使文化事业适应现代化建设的要求,铺设(pūshè, to lay, to pave)小康文化新台阶,最近该市又制定了"九五"文化建设的"创优工程"、"百花工程"、"读书工程"等十大工程。(1996.11.30)

华夏　Huáxià　中国的古称　archaic name for China

三、练　习

(一)**熟读下列词语**:
(1) 粮食　油料　糖料　烤烟　茶叶
(2) 农业是国民经济的基础　家庭联产承包责任制
(3) 乡镇企业　乡村工业
(4) 贫困户　脱贫致富　吃饭问题　温饱问题
(5) 中低产田　低产田　高产田

(二)**请把下列短文译成外语**:

有些人担心,中国人到底能不能养活自己? 对于这个问题,中国政府刚刚发表了粮食问题白皮书(báipíshū, white paper)。中国政府一贯把立足国内资源、实现粮食自给,作为解决粮食问题的基本方针;一直把计划生育(jìhuà shēngyù, family planning)、保护耕地作为基本国策。……实践将再次证明,中国人民不仅能养活自己,而且生活质量还会逐步提高。(1996.11.15)

四、小　知　识
BACKGROUND INFORMATION

(一)家庭联产承包责任制 Household Contracted Responsibility System with Remuneration Linked to Output

这是中国政府在人民公社制度以后,在农村施行的一项新政策,也是一种新的经营方式。即:土地等主要生产资料为国家或集体所有;农民以家庭为单位,承包、经营一定数量的农田,并向国家交纳和出售规定数量的农产品,多余的农产品可自用,也可在集市上出售。各地在实施这一政策时都有一些具体的规定。

It is a post-commune rural policy or a new managerial system that the Chinese Government has adopted. What is stipulated is that the land and other basic means of production belong to the state or the collective; that as an individual household the farmers are entitled to contract to manage a certain amount of farmland from which a fixed number of the products would be sold to the state after the payment of agricultural tax; that the farmers can keep the surplus products for their own consumption or sell them on the market. There are always some specific formulations in implementing this policy in different places.

(二)统分结合的双层经营体制 The Two-Level System of

Combining the Centralized Management with the Decentralized Management

指中国农村实行的统一经营和分散经营两个层次的经营体制,它不同于人民公社时期生产队单一的集中经营体制。家庭承包经营是在集体经济内,在土地等基本生产资料公有的前提下的分散经营层次。统一经营是指乡镇企业和农业社会化服务体系等集体经济的经营层次。中国共产党十三届八中全会指出,今后农村改革的方向:"要继续稳定以家庭联产承包为主的责任制,不断完善统分结合的双层经营体制,积极发展农业社会化服务体系,逐步壮大集体经济的实力。"

This two-level managerial system carried out in the rural areas in China is different from the unitary system of the centralized management on a basis of individual production brigades during the period of communes. The household contracted responsibility system at the decentralized managerial level is in the collective economy with publicly owned farmland and other basic means of production. "Centralized management" here refers to township enterprises and socialized agricultural service system at the collective economic managerial level. At the Eighth Plenary Session of the Thirteenth Central Committee of the Communist Party of China it was decided that the direction of rural reform for the period ahead " is to continually stabilize the responsibility systems led by the household contracts with remuneration linked to output, perfect the two-level managerial system of both centralization and decentralization, actively develop the socialized agricultural service system, and to strengthen, step by step, the collective economy. "

(三)定购 A System of Fixed Quotas for Purchasing

中国对粮、棉、油等属于人民基本生活资料的主要农产品实行定购政策。这就是,国家根据承包合同规定,向农民收购一定数量的粮、棉、油等农产品。国家收购农民在完成定购任务后自愿出售的多余农产品,叫做"议购";议购价格一般高于定购价。

It is a Chinese system to fix quotas with farmers for purchasing their agricultural products such as grain, cotton and oil-basic means of people's livelihood. The state purchasing of farmers' products on a voluntary basis in addition to the fixed quota is known as " a negotiated buy ", often at a higher price than that offered for ordered products.

(四)"丰收计划" "Bumper Harvest Programme"

"丰收计划"是由农业部和财政部共同组织实施的国家级农业科技综合推广计划,它以发展高产、优质、高效农业为目标,有计划有组织地在全国大面积、大范围推广农业科技成果和先进适用技术;从 1986 年开始实施。(据《人民日报》,1996.9.24)

This is a programme jointly organized and implemented by the Ministry of Agriculture and the Ministry of Finance for spreading in an all-round way the state-level agricultural science and technology, with the aim to develop high-yield, high-quality and high-effective agriculture, to spread in a planned and organized way agricultural science and technology results and advanced applicable techniques in a large area and scope throughout China. It was started in 1986.

(taken from the *people's Daily*, 24.9.1996)

第八课　交通、邮电
VIII. TRAFFIC，POST AND TELECOMMUNICATIONS

一、词语和句子

（一）关于交通

航空　（航运）　通航　通车

通道　航线　高速公路

---

(1) 中国西南航空公司承运的成都——曼谷航线于 10 月 28 日正式通航。(1996.10.29)

(2) 连接我国南北的铁路大通道京九铁路提前于今年 9 月 1 日正式开通运营。(1996.9.27)

(3) 对沿江经济带开发与发展有重要作用的上海至南京的高速公路已正式通车。(1996.9.27)

(4) 中韩客货班轮航线开通 6 周年，1.6 万吨级豪华客货轮香雪兰号(Xiāngxuělán Hào)首航青岛。(1996.11.28)

（二）关于运输

客运　货运

列车　客车　货车　　快车　慢车　直达车

---

(1) 近几年来,我国运输市场发生了巨大而深刻的变化。就在新铁路线加快发展的同时,公路、航空、水路的建设规模和运输能力迅猛增长,铁路在运输市场中的份额不断下降:客运已由 65％降至 45％,货运也由 75％降到 55％;今年头 8 个月全路客运量比去年同期又下降了 14％。(1996.11.21)

(2) (铁道部改革方案之一:)优化列车结构,满足市场多层次需求。客车基本上取消了市郊列车和混合列车,直通客车的比重上升到 24.7％;快车的比重占 46.3％,慢车的比重下降到 28.8％。货物列车大幅度增加了集装箱快运直达车次。(1996.11.21)

(3) 新中国第一家中外合资企业——中波轮船公司建立 40 年来,共运载货物 2830 万吨,完成货物周转量 3156 万吨海里,船舶往返于世界各地 100 多个港口,并开辟了集装箱班轮。(1991.6.20)

（三）关于邮电

> 通信网络　通讯卫星　　电讯　电话
> 自动化　普及率

(1) 今后五年里，我国将加快发展长途电话自动化，提高电话普及率，逐步形成方便迅速的通信网络。(1991. 4.12)

(2) 中国和美国之间新的一条电话通道日前正式开通，标志着两国间电讯合作的迅速发展。[中美之间]第一条电话通道是 1973 年建立的，这条电话通道通过太平洋上空的通讯卫星进行联系。(1991.8.5)

(3) 以光缆干线建设为重点的邮电通讯建设，今年继续保持快速发展的良好势头。(1996.9.27)

（四）生　　词

1. 通航	tōngháng	to be open to navigation or air traffic
2. 通车	tōngchē	to be open to traffic
3. 通道	tōngdào	passage way
4. 航线	hángxiàn	air or shipping line, route, course
5. 高速公路	gāosù gōnglù	expressway, freeway

6.	承运	chéngyùn	undertake the transportation of（goods）
7.	开通	kāitōng	to be opened
8.	运营	yùnyíng	(of buses, ships, etc.) run, ply
9.	沿江	yánjiāng	along the river
10.	…带	…dài	zone, area
11.	客货轮	kè-huòlún	passenger-cargo steamer
12.	班轮	bānlún	regular passenger or cargo ship
13.	吨级	dūnjí	tonnage
14.	首航	shǒuháng	maiden voyage or flight
15.	列车	lièchē	train
16.	直达（/通）车	zhídá（/tōng）chē	through train
17.	运输	yùnshū	transport, transportation
18.	份额	fèn'é	share, portion
19.	层次	céngcì	level
20.	需求	xūqiú	need, demand
21.	比重	bǐzhòng	proportion
22.	集装箱	jízhuāngxiāng	container
23.	车次	chēcì	train number
24.	运载	yùnzài	to carry, to deliver
25.	周转量	zhōuzhuǎnliàng	turnover volume
26.	船舶	chuánbó	shipping, boats and ships
27.	往返	wǎngfǎn	go there and home, out and home

28. 港口　　gǎngkǒu　　harbour，port
29. 开辟　　kāipì　　to open up，to start
30. 网络　　wǎngluò　　network
31. 通讯　　tōngxùn　　communication
32. 电讯　　diànxùn　　telecommunication
33. 普及率　pǔjílù　　popularization
34. 光缆　　guānglǎn　　optical cable
35. 干线　　gànxiàn　　main line

（五）专有名词

1. 西南航空　Xīnán Hángkōng　the Southwest Airlines
   公司　　　Gōngsī
2. 成都　　　Chéngdū　　capital city of Sichuan
   　　　　　　　　　　　Province
3. 曼谷　　　Màngǔ　　Bangkok
4. 京九铁路　Jīng-Jiǔ Tiělù　the Beijing-Jiulong
   　　　　　　　　　　　（Kowloon）Railway
5. 南京　　　Nánjīng　　capital city of Jiangsu
   　　　　　　　　　　　Province
6. 韩国　　　Hánguó　　South Korea
7. 中波轮船　Zhōng-Bō Lúnchuán　the Chinese-Polish Joint
   公司　　　Gōngsī　　Stock Shipping Co.
8. 太平洋　　Tàipíngyáng　　Pacific Ocean

二、阅读短文

(一)

长春至四平高速公路建成通车

在国庆节即将来临之际,长春至四平高速公路于 9 月 19 日建成通车。公路全长 133 公里,双向（shuāngxiàng，two-way）四车道（chēdào，roadway）,全封闭（fēngbì，closed）,全立交（lìjiāo，grade separation）,设计时速（shísù，speed per hour）为 120 公里。(1996.9.20)

1. 长春　Chángchūn　capital city of Jilin Province
2. 四平　Sìpíng　a city in Jilin Province

(二)

新疆光缆通信干线开通运行

新疆光缆通信干线 11 月 29 日开通运行,并与已建成开通的亚欧光缆新疆段及 23 条地（dì，prefecture，subprovincial administrative division，也叫地区、专区）、州（zhōu，[autonomous] prefecture）至县的光缆沟通,使新疆光缆通信干线总长达 7600 余公里。投资 4.17 亿元建成的光缆通信干线,近期可提供 3.8 万条长途电路。(1996.12.5)

新疆　Xīnjiāng　　新疆维吾尔自治区　Xinjiang Uygur Autonomous Region（in Northwest China）

三、练　习

(一)熟读下列词语：

(1) 陆上通道　航线开通　首次通航　正式通航　正式通车 全线开工　全面开工　全面建成　完全贯通

(2) 空中通道　电话通道

(3) 机车内燃化　线路电气化　电话自动化　机械化

(4) 铁路线路　重要线路　铁路干线　电话线路　通信线路 主干线

(5) 客运量　客运周转量　货运周转量

(6) 长途快车　短途快车　特别快车　直达快车　定期班车 定期航班

(7) 班机　班车　班轮

(二)请说出京九铁路经过的省名和它们的简称：

1.（北京：京）—[　　：　　]—[　　：　　]—[　　：　　]—[　　：　　]—[　　：　　]—[　　：　　]—[　　：　　]—（九龙： 九）

(三)请把下列短文翻译成外语：

(1)

黑龙江陆海国际联运开通

由黑龙江省绥芬河经俄罗斯东方港至日本、韩国及台湾、香港 等地陆海联运（liányùn，through transport）于日前开通，首批物资已从绥芬河运往东方港。新航道开通后,哈尔滨与日本新舄港的运距可缩短 1600 公里,节省运费近一半。(1996.11.19)

1. 黑龙江 Hēilóng jiāng   a province in Northeast China
2. 绥芬河 Suífēn hé   a city in Heilongjing Province
3. 东方港 Dōngfāng Gǎng   Orient Harbour
4. 哈尔滨 (Hā'ěrbīn) Harbin   capital city of Heilongjiang Province
5. 新舄   Xīnxì   Niigata (a harbour city in Japan)

(2)

大凉山的选择

大凉山,曾经是一片荒凉的山。

如今,这里四通八达的公路、横贯全州的铁路干线、可升降当今世界上最大飞机的航空港、几秒钟就可以拨通全球的通讯网络,以及中国最大的航天火箭(hángtiān huǒjiàn,rocket)发射(fāshè,launch)基地,都表明大凉山已今非昔比。

(大凉山 Dàliángshān 中国少数民族之一彝族的聚居地。行政区域为凉山彝族自治州,属四川省。A region where the Yi nationality live in a compact community. The administrative district is Liangshan Yi Autonomous Prefecture under Sichuan Province.)

四、小 知 识
BACKGROUND INFORMATION

（一）中国的行政区划和"计划单列市" **Chinese Administrative Divisions and "Cities with Economic Planning Directly Supervised by State Council**

中国的省级行政区域有 33 个：23 个省、4 个直辖市、5 个民族自治区、1 个特别行政区。直辖市的城区分为若干区，郊区为县。省和自治区下为地区（在民族自治地方为"自治州"或"盟"），或地级市；地区及地级市下为县，或县级市（在民族自治地方为"自治县"、"旗"或"自治旗"，有些"特区"、"工农区"、"林区"也是县级行政地区）。直辖市以外的某些大中城市也有"区"的设置。县以下为乡或镇。

China has 33 administrative divisions at provincial level：23 provinces， four municipalities directly under the Central Government， five autonomous regions for minority nationalities and one special administrative region. In a municipality directly under the Central Government the urban area is divided into different districts and the outskirts are divided into different counties. Under a province or an autonomous region are different prefectures (autonomous prefectures or league correspondingly) and prefectural municipalities. Under a prefecture or a prefectural municipality are counties (or autonomous counties， banners， autonomous banners， some special zones， industrial agricultural zones and forest zones of county level) and corresponding towns. Some big cities other than those directly under the Central Government also have administrative divisions of " districts". A county is formed by villages and towns.

设立计划单列市是经济管理体制上的措置，即若干大中城市在不改变省辖市行政隶属关系的情况下，被赋予相当于省一级的经济管理权限。这些城市的经济和社会发展计划不再经由所在省下达，而在国家计划中单独立户，其主要计划直接上报国家有关部门，国家的若干计划指标直接下达这些城市执行。从 1983 年到 1990 年 6 月，国务院先后批准 14 个城市实行计划单列。

Cities with economic planning directly supervised by the State Council is regarded as an economic managerial measure. It refers to some big or medium cities that are authorized to perform the duty of a province in terms of the economic management without changing the jurisdiction of the province they are under. Their municipal plans for economic and social development are not to be conveyed by the province. As a specifically designated city，they can send their major plans directly to the state departments concerned，and on the other hand，be assigned some to be fulfilled. Between 1983 and June 1990 the State Council granted 14 cities their request for economic planning directly supervised by the State Council.

（二）关于中国地名的简称 Abbreviations for Chinese Place Names

中国地名一般都有简称；多用于报纸标题和交通线的名称上。它们是：

There are abbreviations for almost every Chinese place name. They are often used in newspaper headlines or names of the main communications artery.

大陆 32 个省级行政区的简称——

The following are the abbreviations for the municipalities directly under the Central Government：

（直辖市）

北京：京	天津：津	上海：沪 Hù、申 Shēn
京 for 北京	津 for 天津	沪 or 申 for 上海
重庆：渝（Yú）		
渝 for 重庆		

The Following are the abbreviations for the provinces：

（省）	河北：冀 Jì	山东：鲁 Lǔ	山西：晋 Jìn
	冀 for 河北	鲁 for 山东	晋 for 山西
	辽宁：辽	吉林：吉	黑龙江：黑
	辽 for 辽宁	吉 for 吉林	黑 for 黑龙江

93

江苏:苏、江　　浙江:浙　　　安徽:皖 Wǎn
苏 or 江 for 江苏　浙 for 浙江　　皖 for 安徽
福建:闽 Mǐn　　河南:豫 Yù　　湖北:鄂 È
闽 for 福建　　　豫 for 河南　　鄂 for 湖北
湖南:湘 Xiāng　　江西:赣 Gàn　　广东:粤 Yuè
湘 for 湖南　　　赣 for 江西　　粤 for 广东
陕西:陕、秦 Qín　甘肃:甘、陇 Lǒng　青海:青
陕 or 秦 for 陕西　甘 or 陇 for 甘肃　青 for 青海
四川:川、蜀 Shǔ　云南:云、滇 Diān　贵州:贵、黔 Qián
川 or 蜀 for 四川　云 or 滇 for 云南　贵 or 黔 for 贵州
海南:琼 Qióng
琼 for 海南

The following are the abbreviations for the autonomous regions:

（自治区）

内蒙古自治区:内蒙　　新疆维吾尔自治区:新
内蒙 for 内蒙古自治区　新 for 新疆维吾尔自治区
宁夏回族自治区:宁　　西藏自治区:藏
宁 for 宁夏回族自治区　藏 for 西藏自治区
广西壮族自治区:桂
桂 for 广西壮族自治区

The following is the abbreviation for the special administrative region:

（特别行政区）香港:港
　　　　　港 for 香港

　此外——The following are the abbreviations for Macao and Taiwan:

澳门:澳　　台湾:台
澳 for 澳门　台 for 台湾

城市除北京、天津、上海、重庆 4 个直辖市外,常见的简称还有:

The following are the abbreviations for cities other than Beijing, Tianjin, Shanghai and Chongqing:

哈尔滨:哈	沈阳:沈	大连:大
哈 for 哈尔滨	沈 for 沈阳	大 for 大连
青岛:青	大同:大	南京:宁 Níng
青 for 青岛	大 for 大同	宁 for 南京
南昌:南	福州:福、榕 Róng	武汉:汉
南 for 南昌	福 or 榕 for 福州	汉 for 武汉
广州:广、穗 Suì	深圳:深	兰州:兰
广 or 穗 for 广州	深 for 深圳	兰 for 兰州
成都:成、蓉 Róng	昆明:昆	秦皇岛:秦
成 or 蓉 for 成都	昆 for 昆明	秦 for 秦皇岛
杭州:杭		
杭 for 杭州		

第九课　商　　业
IX. COMMERCE

一、词语和句子

（一）关于物价

物价总水平　商品零售价格　居民消费价格

（1）8 月份物价总水平有所回升。城市物价受灾害影响，商品零售价格和居民消费价格分别比上月上涨1.4％和 1.7％，涨幅高于农村 0.2 和 0.4 个百分点。（1996.9.17）

（2）价格结构的调整要充分考虑企业和居民的承受能力，着眼于促进经济结构的调整和企业效益的提高。（1991.1.14）

(二)关于市场

社会消费零售总额
市场供应　购销两旺　供求平衡　供不应求
供过于求　花色品种
商场　供销社　代销店　集贸市场　个体户

---

(1) ("九五"计划第一年的)前九个月,社会消费零售总额
比上年同期增长 19.7%,扣除价格因素,实际增长
12.3%。物价涨幅持续稳定地回落到较低水平。
(1996.11.19)

(2) 根据商业部对 705 种主要商品供求情况的分析,下半
年供不应求的商品为 86 种,占 12.2%,与上半年相
比,紧缺面缩小 3.7 个百分点;供求基本平衡的商品
426 种,占 60.4%,比上半年上升 1.7 个百分点;供过
于求的商品 193 种,占 27.4%,上升 2 个百分点。
(1991.7.15)

(3) 1990 年我国猪肉、蔬菜市场供应好于往年,购销两
旺,花色品种增加,购销价格基本平稳。今年国家还将
在丰富居民"菜篮子"方面下更大的工夫。(1991.1.
28)

(4) 目前,农村形成了多种所有制并存的商业格局——县
城较大商场、乡镇基层供销社、村代销店以及各类集
贸市场和个体户的格局。(1996.11.26)

（三）关于人民生活

居民　支出　储蓄余额　人均生活费　人均收入
耐用消费品　生产资料

(1) 城乡居民收入大幅度增长，生活质量提高。扣除物价因素，城镇居民人均生活费收入年均增长 7.7％，农民人均收入增长 4.5％。（1996.11.15）

(2) 据对辽宁省农村 1890 个农户调查，1996 年 1—9 月份农民人均生活消费支出为 897.32 元，比去年同期增长 29.5％。（1996.11.24）

(3) 农民购买大件耐用消费品愿意到较大城市较大商店中购买。因为在这些商店中商品相对丰富，可挑选的余地大，另外售后服务也更完善。而农用生产资料，农民一般都愿在就近的供销社系统的商店购买，农民反映这里"货真价实"。（1996.11.26）

(4) 因为不知道再该买什么，一些富裕起来的农民只好把钱存在银行里。［在一个比较贫困的县里，］1995 年人均纯收入 1393 元，但农业银行的储蓄余额为 1.8 亿元。（1996.11.25）

（四）生　词

1. 消费　　xiāofèi　　　　　consume
2. 回升　　huíshēng　　　　rise again (after a fall),

			pick up
3.	灾害	zāihài	calamity，disaster
4.	分别	fēnbié	respectively，separately
5.	上涨	shàngzhǎng	to go up，to rise
6.	涨幅	zhǎngfú	rate of（price）rise
7.	调整	tiáozhěng	to regulate，to adjust
8.	承受	chéngshòu	to bear，to endure
9.	着眼于	zháoyǎn yú	to have something in mind
10.	供应	gōngyìng	to supply
11.	购销两旺	gòu xiāo liǎng wàng	brisk buying and selling
12.	供求	gōngqiú	supply and demand
13.	平衡	pínghéng	balance
14.	供不应求	gōng bù yìng qiú	demand exceeds supply
15.	供过于求	gōng guò yú qiú	supply exceeds demand
16.	花色	huāsè	（of merchandise）variety of designs，sizes，colours，etc.
17.	品种	pǐnzhǒng	variety，assortment
18.	供销社	gōngxiāoshè	supply and marketing cooperative
19.	代销店	dàixiāodiàn	commission agent
20.	集贸市场	jímào shìchǎng	market
21.	个体户	gètǐhù	individual household，self-employed businessman
22.	扣除	kòuchú	to deduct
23.	因素	yīnsù	factor

24. 紧缺	jǐnquē	in short supply，in urgent demand
25. 菜篮子	càilánzi	"shopping or vegetable basket"，nonstaple food
26. 格局	géjú	pattern
27. 支出	zhīchū	expenses；expenditure
28. 储蓄	chǔxù	saving deposit
29. 余额	yú'é	balance remaining sum
30. 耐用	nàiyòng	durable
31. 生产资料	shēngchǎn zīliào	means of production
32. 售后服务	shòuhòu fúwù	aftersales service
33. 货真价实	huò zhēn jià shí	genuine goods at a fair price

二、阅读短文

（一）

农民想要买点啥？

一些从温饱型走向小康型生活水平的农民说，现在不是买啥买不到，而是不知道再该买点啥。

辽宁省本溪市一个农民告诉记者，他和他的儿女家中，彩电、电冰箱、摩托车……，几乎应有尽有，下一步就不知道再该买什么好了。他们说，70 年代有老"三大件"：手表、自行车、缝纫机。80 年代有新"三大件"：电视机、电冰箱、洗衣机。到了 90 年代却未见新的"三大件"问世（wènshì, to come out），缺少能刺激（cìjī, to stimulate）农民进一步消费的增长点。由于没啥可买，一些富裕起来的农民只好把钱存在银行里。在辽宁一个比较贫困的县，今年 1—9 月份，储蓄余额比去年同期增加了 2870 万元。

开拓农村市场，需要工商企业真正深入农村，了解农民需求，这样，富裕起来的农民才不会"没啥可买"。（1996.11.26）

（二）

菜篮充盈看供求

日前,记者从农业部门获悉[huòxī，to learn（of an event）]，今年全国禽（qín，fowl）、肉、蛋、奶、水产品、果蔬全面丰收,"菜篮子"产品稳步增长,产销两旺。……

"菜篮子"产品的发展和市场供应的改善,为实现治理通货膨胀为目标的宏观调控（tiáokòng，control）作出了积极的贡献。今年前三季度,食品类价格比上年同期上涨 8.6%,涨幅回落 20.2 个百分点,影响价格总水平回落 7.8 个百分点。即,在同期社会商品零售价格总水平回落的 10 个百分点中,有 3/4 是食品价格回落的功劳。可见,"菜篮子工程"的实施,确实起了保障供给,稳定物价的作用。（1996.12.18）

三、练 习

（一）熟读下列词语：

（1）物价总水平 商品零售价格 居民消费价格

（2）市场供应 市场销售 购销两旺 供不应求 供过于求

（3）生活质量 居民收入 人均收入 消费支出 生活费

储蓄余额
（4）耐用消费品　生活资料　生产资料

（二）请把下列短文译成外语：

今年农村经济全面发展
粮食总产量可超过 4800 亿公斤　农民人均收入增长 5％左右

　　记者从全国农业工作会议上获悉，今年我国农业生产再获丰收，农民收入继续增加，农村经济全面发展。粮食在去年较大幅度增产的基础上，再创历史最高水平，预计总产量可超过 4800 亿公斤，比上年增产 135 亿公斤以上。棉花和油料受多种因素影响，有所减产，但供给仍可满足需求。"菜篮子"产品持续增长，预计肉类总产量 5800 万吨，水产品总产量 2800 万吨，分别比去年增长 10.3％和 11.2％，禽蛋、奶类、蔬菜、水果等也都比上年有较大幅度增产。乡镇企业运行平稳，速度和效益适度增长，预计增加值比上年增长 16.5％。全年农业增加值预计比去年增长 4.5％左右，农民人均收入比上年实际增长 5％左右。（1996.12.20）

四、小　知　识
BACKGROUND INFORMATION

（一）关于报纸的标题 The Headlines of a Newspaper
　　报纸的标题除了正题外，有时还有眉题和副题，眉题在正题上面，副题在正题下面，分别用不同的字体和字号标出；正题突出新闻的主题，字体较庄重，字号较大，地位显著。副题有时不止一个，副题之外，还有内容提要。如：

中共十三届八中全会在京举行

中央政治局主持会议　江泽民作重要讲话
审议通过《中共中央关于进一步加强农业和农村工作的决定》
确定党的十四大于明年第四季度在北京举行

全会充分肯定十一届三中全会以来党在农村的各项基本政策,高度评价八十年代我国农村改革和建设所取得的巨大成就。全会指出,全党同志要充分认识农业在实现国民经济和社会发展第二步战略目标中的重要地位和作用,下更大的决心,采取切实有力的措施,加强农业这个基础,全面完成十年规划和"八五"计划确定的农业发展目标和任务,逐步使广大农民的生活从温饱达到小康水平。

国务院最近决定
部分商品物资将降价销售
让利四十亿元左右降幅控制在百分之二十以内

以邓小平理论和党的十五大精神为指导　对解决金融改革和发展中重大问题作具体部署
全国金融工作会议在京召开
江泽民李鹏朱镕基作重要讲话　胡锦涛李岚清等出席

●金融是现代经济的核心。进一步做好金融工作,保证金融安全、高效、稳健运行,是国民经济持续快速健康发展的基本条件

●必须以邓小平理论和党的十五大精神为指导,按照建立社会主义市场经济体制的方向,深化和加快金融改革

●力争用3年左右时间大体建立与社会主义市场经济发展相适应的金融机构体系、金融市场体系和金融调控监管体系,显著提高金融业经营和管理水平,基本实现全国金融秩序明显好转

●必须根据社会主义市场经济发展的要求,强化人民银行的金融监管职能,加快国有商业银行的商业化步伐

●必须依法治理金融,规范和维护社会主义市场经济的金融秩序,大力整章建制,严厉惩治金融犯罪和违法违规活动,把一切金融活动纳入规范化、法制化的轨道

●必须加快经济体制和经济增长方式两个根本转变,为金融良性循环创造好的经济环境,特别是要加快国有企业改革,建立政企分开的投资体制,加大经济结构调整力度,坚决避免"大而全、小而全"和不合理重复建设

李鹏与博尔格会谈
双方就发展中新友好合作关系及共同关心的问题达成广泛共识

104

In a Chinese newspaper a headline is sometimes crowned with an upper subheading and supported by a lower subheading. All the headings are printed in types of different style and size. The main heading is the topic of a news item, therefore it is always printed in solemn and bold types and prominently featured. Sometimes there is an additional subheading followed by a summary of the news report.

(二)统销 Planned Marketing by the State

统一销售、供应。中国政府为保证国家建设和人民生活对粮食和主要农产品的需要,从 1953 年起,实行统一收购,统一销售、供应的政策;1955 年 8 月颁布了有关规定。直到几年前,中国城镇居民的粮油等一直由国家按统一价格有计划地凭证供应。

It means "unified selling". To guarantee the supply of grain and staple agricultural products needed in the state construction and people's livelihood, the Chinese Government began a policy of planned purchase, marketing and supply of the above-mentioned agricultural products since 1953. The documents in detail were issued in August 1955. Until a few years ago, the Chinese townspeople were supplied with grain, oil and other foodstuffs by the state according to their residence cards at a unified price in a planned way.

(三)"搭车"涨价、"菜篮子"及其它 Raise Prices by "Getting a Lift", "the Vegetable Basket", etc.

"搭车"原意是搭乘车子。"'搭车'涨价"是一种比喻,意思是利用国家调高某些商品价格的机会,把不属于调价的商品也跟着涨价出售。

搭车 means "by car" or "get a lift". '搭车' 涨价 (raise prices by "getting a lift") is used in a figurative sense, referring to those businessmen who have raised the price of some unlisted goods by taking advantage of the Government's price readjustment.

"菜篮子"原意是居民采购副食品的篮子,这里是指居民的副食品需要。中国正在实施的"菜篮子"工程是在大中城市郊区建设生产基地,增加副食品生产,以供应市场,满足城乡居民的需要。

菜篮子 originally means "a shopping basket of non-staple food", referring figuratively to the townspeople's need for non-staple food. A "vegetable basket project" is being carried out in China to construct production bases in the outskirts of big or medium-sized cities and increase the production of non-staple food for the market, so as to meet the requirements of the urban residents.

在汉语中,人们常常利用各种修辞手段,对一些较抽象的概念赋予形象化的说法,在读报时,要弄清它们的实际含意。下面再介绍几个常见的说法:

In Chinese a figure of speech is often used to describe an abstract concept. Newspaper readers should work out its exact meaning when they come across a simile or metaphor. There are some more examples below.

大锅饭(dàguōfàn):1958 年中国农村的人民公社化运动中,办起了很多公共食堂,人们都在食堂吃饭,叫做"吃大锅饭"。"吃大锅饭"忽视了人们不同的实际情况,也造成了极大的浪费,后来得到了纠正。现在,"大锅饭"、"吃大锅饭"用来指分配上的平均主义,即不管劳动者技能的高低、贡献的大小,都给予大体上相同的报酬。

大锅饭(food prepared in a big canteen cauldron):The phrase

吃大锅饭 was used to describe the commune members who ate in one canteen in the rural areas during the period of the communes in 1958. This arrangement was regardless of different conditions and too much waste of food, and was corrected later. Now the phrases of 大锅饭 and 吃大锅饭 are often used to describe the equalitarianist payment irrespective of one's skills and contribution.

铁饭碗(tiěfànwǎn)："饭碗"本用来比喻人们赖以领取报酬、维持生活来源的职业岗位。"铁"比喻其稳定、可靠,无失业之虞。"铁饭碗"指劳动者一旦进入某一工作岗位,就有了可靠的工资收入,不管是否称职,一律不能辞退、解雇。这是中国国营企业、事业单位长期实行的一种劳动制度,现正加以逐步改革。

铁饭碗(an iron rice bowl)：饭碗 originally refers to one's work or post——source of income. 铁 means "secure", "reliable" or "without any worries about losing one's job". As a figure of speech,铁饭碗 carries a meaning of "one's employment is a secure source of income without any danger of being dismissed even if one is incompetent". This is a true description of the labour system which was carried out in China's state enterprises and institutions over a long period of time and is now undergoing a gradual reform.

一刀切(yīdāoqiē)：指制定、执行政策时,不作调查研究,不管具体对象的差别,都一律对待。

一刀切(cut with one knife)：It figuratively refers to an equal application of one policy to different people or things without necessary investigation.

土政策(tǔzhèngcè)：人们常常把某一地区、单位内部制定、实施的,不符合中央政策规定和精神的政策、规定、办法叫"土政策"。

土政策 (a local policy)：The policies, regulations and measures formulated by and implemented in a region or an organization in disagreement with the relevant policies, regulations or measures adopted by the Central Government are known as a "local policy".

第十课 对外贸易与经济合作
X. FOREIGN TRADE AND ECONOMIC COOPERATION

一、词语和句子

（一）关于对外贸易

对外贸易总额 进出口总值 进/出口［额］

国际支付能力 外汇储备 汇率

一般贸易 加工贸易

---

(1) 截至 10 月份,全国累计进出口总值已达 2264.3 亿美元,增长 2.5%。其中出口 1192.2 亿美元,与去年同期基本持平;进口 1072.1 亿美元,增长 5.5%,增长速度持续回落。累计顺差 120.1 亿美元。(1996.11.13)

(2) 9 月份,我国外贸进出口总额为 237.1 亿美元。其中一般贸易进出口额比上月均有所减少,加工贸易仍在进出口贸易中占据主导地位,外商投资企业进出口增长迅速。(1996.10.16)

(3) [七五期间]我国贸易收支保持良好状态,国际支付能力增强。(1991.1.24)

(4) 李鹏总理在第80届广交会开幕式上说,我们预计,到2000年,中国对外贸易总额将达到4000亿美元,进出口总额将保持平衡,中国将为世界各国提供一个广阔的市场。(1996.10.16)

(5) 新出台的改革方案,主要是在已经调整人民币汇率的基础上,建立外贸企业自负盈亏机制。(1991.1.24)

(6) 中国将进一步扩大对外经济技术合作,要在保有一定外汇储备的情况下,本着"进出口基本平衡"的原则,相应增加进口。中国不搞贸易保护主义。(1991.6.4)

(二)关于经济合作

三资企业	国际合作	国际惯例	国际竞争
投资环境	投资法规	投资项目	投资金额

(1) 联合国官员说,总的来说,中国提供了良好的投资环境,其中最重要的是政治稳定为外国投资创造了有利条件。此外,中国政府还尽最大努力不断完善有关投资法规。(1991.7.22)

（2）截至今年 6 月,累计批准外商直接投资项目近 27 万个,实际使用外资金额 1500 多亿美元,已开业的三资企业逾 12 万家。最近 3 年连续成为除美国以外吸引外资最多的国家。(1996.9.5)

（3）在[今年上半年]批准的外商投资企业中,中外合资企业三千二百二十四家,协议金额二十五点二九亿美元;合作企业六百七十一家,协议金额七点八五亿美元;独资企业一千一百二十八家,协议金额十一点九二亿美元。(1991.7.27.海外)

（4）在未来的五年计划中,中国航空工业将加大力度更大范围地开展国际经济技术合作,积极向国际惯例靠拢,以参与国际竞争。(1996.11.7)

（5）我们建立了深圳、珠海、厦门、汕头、海南 5 个经济特区,它们已经形成相当的规模,取得了巨大的成就。(1991.5.13)

（三）生　词

1. 对外贸易　duìwài màoyì　foreign trade
2. 支付　　　zhīfù　　　　to pay, to defray
3. 外汇　　　wàihuì　　　 foreign exchange
4. 储备　　　chǔbèi　　　 reserve store
5. 汇率　　　huìlǜ　　　　exchange rate
6. 一般贸易　yībān màoyì　general trade

7. 加工贸易　jiāgōng màoyì　　processing trade
8. 截至　　　jiézhì　　　　　　by (a specified time), up to
9. 持平　　　chípíng　　　　　to balance
10. 顺差　　　shùnchā　　　　　favourable balance
11. 外商　　　wàishāng　　　　foreign businessman
12. 投资　　　tóuzī　　　　　　to invest
13. 占据　　　zhànjù　　　　　to occupy, to hold
14. 收支　　　shōuzhī　　　　　revenue and expenditure, income and expenses
15. …式　　　…shì　　　　　　type, style
16. 出台　　　chūtái　　　　　to put out, to put in force
17. 方案　　　fāng'àn　　　　　scheme, programme
18. 本着　　　běnzhe　　　　　in line with
19. 贸易保护　màoyì bǎohù　　protectionism
　　主义　　　zhǔyì
20. 惯例　　　guànlì　　　　　convention, usual practice
21. 法规　　　fǎguī　　　　　　laws and regulations
22. 金额　　　jīn'é　　　　　　amount of money
23. 官员　　　guānyuán　　　　official
24. 外资　　　wàizī　　　　　foreign capital or fund
25. 开业　　　kāiyè　　　　　to start business
26. 逾　　　　yú　　　　　　　to exceed, to go beyond
27. 吸引　　　xīyǐn　　　　　to attract
28. 规模　　　guīmó　　　　　scale, scope
29. 靠拢　　　kàolǒng　　　　to draw close, to close up

112

30. 特区　　　tèqū　　　　　　special zone

（四）专有名词

1. 深圳　　Shēnzhèn　　a city in Guangdong Province
2. 珠海　　Zhūhǎi　　　a city in Guangdong Province
3. 厦门　　Xiàmén　　　a city in Fujian Province
4. 汕头　　Shàntóu　　a city in Guangdong Province

二、阅读短文

世行说中国经济形势很好

　　新华社华盛顿 5 月 29 日电　世界银行 28 日发表一份有关中国的专题报告说，1996 年中国经济发展形势很好，但为了保持高速、低通胀（tōngzhàng，inflation）的经济增长，还须深化改革。

　　报告指出，1995 年，中国成功地把通胀率降到了 15％以下，并使经济增长率保持在 10％以上。外国直接投资达 380 亿美元，外汇储备已逾 730 亿美元。

　　世行报告认为，1996 年中国力争把通胀率降到 10％以下，并使经济增长速度维持在 8％到 9％，目前形势不错。

　　世行认为，中国要在保持经济高速增长的情况下不引发通货膨胀，应进一步促进国营企业和金融（jīnróng，finance，banking）部门面向市场，重视政府财政支出向诸如（zhūrú，such as）医疗卫生、教育、减少贫困、基础设施建设和环境保护等优先项目的倾向。（1996.5.31）

世界银行　　　shìjiè yínháng　　　the World Bank

三、练 习

(一)熟读下列词语：

    (1) 进出口贸易　进出口总值　进出口平衡

        进口贸易　进口额　进口货物　出口贸易　出口额　出口创汇

        国际支付能力　人民币汇率　外汇储备

    (2) 投资环境　投资项目　投资金额

        合资企业　合作企业　独资企业

        经济特区　沿海开放城市　沿海经济开放区

(二)请把下列短文译成外语：

社论：

进一步加强亚太地区经济合作(节录)

    亚太经合组织成员间经济发展程度有很大不同，人均国民生产总值最高与最低间相差在几十倍以上。只有大力加强经济技术合作，才能为发展中成员(chéngyuán, member)创造更多的发展机会，并扩大市场，使他们逐步缩小与发达成员间的经济差距。因此，采取切实措施，加快经济技术合作步伐，既是发展中成员的要求，也有利于发达成员的经济发展。

    在本次会议上，江主席郑重(zhèngzhòng, solemnly)宣布，今年中国进口商品的平均税率(shuìlù, tax rate)已从原来的 35.9%下降到 23%，到 2000 年争取再下降到 15%左右。所有这些，充分显示了我国推进亚太区域经济合作的诚意。(1996.11.26)

四、小 知 识
BACKGROUND INFORMATION

（一）经济特区和中国的经济开放格局 Special Economic Zones and China's Economic Open Pattern

经济特区指在一个国家和地区划出一定范围，在对外经济活动中采取特殊政策的地区。目前世界上的经济特区已有数百个，遍及 70 多个国家；其中三分之二在发展中国家，三分之一在发达国家。设立经济特区的目的是吸收外国投资，利用国内劳动力，发展在国际市场上有竞争能力的加工出口工业。1980 年 5 月，中国决定在广东省的深圳、珠海、汕头和福建省的厦门，各划出一定范围的区域，试办经济特区，1988 年，又辟海南全省为经济特区。在特区内，在维护主权、法律的原则下，实行优惠政策，引进一些技术密集、知识密集的企业，作为世界先进生产技术、先进管理办法的窗口。1984 年 4 月，中国进一步开放大连、秦皇岛、天津、烟台、青岛、连云港、南通、上海、宁波、温州、福州、广州、湛江、北海 14 个沿海港口城市，并先后开辟了 13 个经济技术开发区和长江三角洲、珠江三角洲、闽南三角地区，以及山东半岛、辽东半岛经济开放区。1990 年又决定开放、开发上海浦东新区。从而形成了"经济特区——沿海开放城市——沿海经济开放区——内地"的逐步推进的对外开放格局。

"Special economic zones" are the country-or region-designated zones where special economic policies are implemented in terms of foreign trade. It is estimated that in the world some hundreds of such zones have been established in over 70 countries. Of the zones two thirds are in the developing countries, and one third in developed countries. What they aim at is to draw foreign investment, make use of their domestic labour force and to develop the competitive export processing industry. In May 1980 the Chinese Government decided to designate special zones for this purpose, i. e. Shenzhen, Zhuhai and Shantou of the Guangdong Province, and Xiamen of the Fujian Province (in 1988 the Hainan Province was specially designated as another economic zone). On the principle of defending state sovereignty and law, favourable policies are implemented there, so as to introduce some high-tech enterprises as a show window of the advanced world-level technology and management. In April 1984 China further opened 14 port cities along the coast to the outside world. They are Dalian, Qinhuangdao, Tianjin, Yantai, Qingdao, Lianyungang, Nantong, Shanghai, Ningbo, Wenzhou, Fuzhou, Guangzhou, Zhanjiang and Beihai. In addition to these cities are 13 zones for economic and technological development together with the Changjiang (Yangtse) River Delta, the Zhujiang (Pearl) River Delta and the Southern Fujian Delta, and economic open regions such as the Shandong Peninsula and the East Liaoning Peninsula. In 1990 a decision was made to open and develop Pudong in Shanghai. Special economic Zones—coastal open cities—coastal economic open regions — the interior: that's how China's open pattern is formed.

(二)广交会 The Guangzhou Export Commodities Fair

中国创办最早、规模最大、层次最高的中国出口商品交易会,由中国对外贸易公司和有关单位联合举办的定期交易会。自1957年起,每年春秋两季在广州举行,简称广交会。除广交会外,中国的商品交易会还有:哈尔滨交易会、上海交易会、西安交易会、乌鲁木

117

齐交易会、大连交易会、昆明交易会等。各省市以及各大城市也举办不同类型的交易会。

It is the earliest, largest and top-level Chinese export commodities fair regularly held by the China National Foreign Trade Corporation and other organizations concerned. After 1957 the Fair is held in spring and autumn in Guangzhou, twice every year; and shortened as 广交会. Beside this fair, other Chinese export commodities fairs include the Harbin Commodities Fair, the Shanghai Commodities Fair, the Xi'an Commodities Fair, the Urumqi Commodities Fair, the Dalian Commodities Fair, the Kunming Commodities Fair, etc. Other commodities fairs in various forms are also held in all provincial capitals and large cities.

第十一课　教育、科技、文化
XI. EDUCATION，SCIENCE AND TECHNOLOGY，CULTURE

一、词语和句子

（一）关于教育

1：面向现代化　面向世界　面向未来（三个"面向"）
社会主义建设者　社会主义接班人

（1）我们必须以面向现代化、面向世界、面向未来的战略
眼光，规划和部署今后 10 年教育事业的发展和改革。
坚持教育的社会主义方向，把培养社会主义的建设者
和接班人作为学校的根本任务。（1991.1.25）

（2）各地区各部门都要十分重视和支持教育事业，贯彻实
施科教兴国战略，推动我国社会和经济的持续发展。
（1996.9.11）

2：基础教育　职业教育　高等教育　成人教育
德智体全面发展

(1) 中国依靠自己的力量已经在十一个学科门类培养了十八万名硕士,十个学科门类培养了七千多名博士。他们中绝大多数已经成为教育和科研的骨干,在基础理论研究、高技术领域和经济主战场上发挥着重要作用。(1991.7.31.海外)

(2) 未来的 15 年,中国将要进入一个崭新的发展时期。在我国,将实现科教兴国和可持续发展战略,教育战线面临艰巨而繁重的任务。各类学校,包括基础教育、职业教育、高等教育和成人教育都要认真贯彻党的教育方针,就是德智体全面发展、培养社会主义事业的建设者和接班人。(1996.9.11)

(二)关于科技

科学技术　科学技术现代化　科学技术的竞争
第一生产力　劳动者素质

(1) 坚持科学技术是第一生产力,把经济建设真正转移到依靠科技进步和提高劳动者素质的轨道上来,是一场广泛而深刻的变革。(1991.5.24)

(2) 国际间的竞争,说到底是综合国力的竞争,关键是科学技术的竞争。(1991.7.25)

(3) 在当今的发达国家,科技进步在经济增长诸因素中的比例达 50—70%,而我们目前还只占 25% 左右。[出席人大和政协会议的]科学家们的一致意见是,必须下定决心,创造各种条件,让科学技术在经济建设的舞台上大显身手。(1991.4.8)

(三)关于文化

《讲话》 "二为"方向 "双百"方针
文艺工作者 社会主义文艺

(1) 为纪念毛泽东同志的《在延安文艺座谈会上的讲话》发表 49 周年,中宣部文艺局与本报文艺部今天共同召开座谈会。与会同志认为,文艺工作者要坚持《讲话》精神,把《讲话》精神落到实处。(1991.5.18)

(2) 我国文艺工作者要坚持"二为"方向和"双百"方针,以饱满的热情讴歌我们伟大的时代和伟大的人民,为繁荣社会主义文艺做出新的贡献。(1996.10.11)

(3) 金鸡百花电影节是我国电影界一年一度的盛大节日。据介绍,本届电影节还将举行第十六届中国电影金鸡奖、第十九届百花奖颁奖典礼。(1996.10.11)

（三）生 词

1. 接班人　　jiēbānrén　　　　successor
2. 眼光　　　yǎnguāng　　　　eye，sight
3. 部署　　　bùshǔ　　　　　disposition，arrangement
4. 硕士　　　shuòshì　　　　master's（degree）
5. 博士　　　bóshì　　　　　doctor's（degree）
6. 骨干　　　gǔgàn　　　　　backbone，mainstay
7. 德智体　　dé zhì tǐ　　　　moral，intellectual and
　　　　　　　　　　　　　　physical development
8. 学科　　　xuékē　　　　　a branch of learning，
　　　　　　　　　　　　　　discipline
9. 门类　　　ménlèi　　　　　class，category
10. 高技术　　gāojìshù　　　　high technology
11. 领域　　　lǐngyù　　　　　field，sphere
12. 主战场　　zhǔzhànchǎng　　main battlefield
13. 崭新　　　zhǎnxīn　　　　brand-new，completely
　　　　　　　　　　　　　　new
14. 可持续　　kě-chíxù fāzhǎn　sustainable development
　　 发展
15. 面临　　　miànlín　　　　to be faced or confronted
　　　　　　　　　　　　　　with
16. 生产力　　shēngchǎnlì　　productive power
17. 轨道　　　guǐdào　　　　track，footing

18. 变革	biàngé	change and reform
19. 说到底	shuōdàodǐ	in the final analysis, at bottom
20. 综合	zōnghé	comprehensive, synthetically
21. 诸	zhū	all, various
22. 舞台	wǔtái	state, arena
23. 大显身手	dà xiǎn shēnshǒu	to distinguish oneself, to give full play to one's abilities
24. "二为"方向	"èr wèi" fāngxiàng	the Direction of "Two Services"
25. "双百"方针	"shuāng bǎi" fāngzhēn	the "Double-Hundred" Policy
26. 文艺	wényì	literature and art
27. 与会	yùhuì	to participate in a conference
28. 实处	shíchù	actual or concrete part
29. 讴歌	ōugē	to sing the praises of, to eulogize
30. …界	jiè	circles
31. 颁奖	bānjiǎng	to award a prize
32. 典礼	diǎnlǐ	ceremony

二、阅读短文

(一)

希望工程在西藏开花结果

西藏青少年发展基金会秘书长告诉记者,希望工程在西藏实施四年来,已累计筹资 3000 多万元,建立希望小学 100 所;累计投入救助(jiùzhù, scour, help)资金近 3000 万元,救助失学儿童 7000 人。目前,8000 多名学生在已建希望小学就读。希望工程有力地促进了西藏乡村基础教育的发展,对加强全区社会主义精神文明建设产生深远影响。(1996.11.22)

青少年发展基金会　Qīng-Shàonián Fāzhǎn Jījīnhuì　the Young People's Development Foundation

（二）

"八五"攻关计划创经济效益逾 600 亿元

"八五"科技攻关（gōngguān，to tackle key problems）计划已圆满完成，累计取得直接经济效益 600 亿元。

五年来，十万科技大军团结协作，共获得科技成果 6 万多项，达到国际先进水平的占 35％，国内领先（lǐngxiān，to be in the lead）水平的占 36％，新产品、新工艺 5000 项，新材料近 3000 种。攻关的大部分成果已在和正在经济建设中推广应用，为推动我国物质文明和精神文明建设作出了巨大贡献。（1996.10.21）

（三）

文艺界部分人士座谈六中全会决议精神

文艺工作者要当好"人类灵魂工程师"

在今天召开的文艺界部分知名人士学习贯彻十四届六中全会精神座谈会上，与会作家、艺术家表示，六中全会为繁荣社会主义文艺指明了方向，文艺工作者应该像《决议》指出的那样，做"人类灵魂工程师"，把最好的精神食粮贡献给人民。

与会者充分肯定文艺界的成就和大好形势，也对那种淡漠（dànmò，be indifferent to）"二为"方向、远离群众实践、推崇（tuīchóng，to hold in esteem）腐朽（fǔxiǔ，decadent）文艺思潮、"一切向钱看"的倾向提出了批评。（1996.11.6）

三、练　　习

（一）熟读下列词语：

　（1）面向现代化　面向世界　面向未来

　　　社会主义建设者　社会主义接班人

126

（2）学士　硕士　博士　博士后

普及教育　义务教育

初等教育　中等教育　高等教育

基础教育　职业教育　成人教育

思想教育　国情教育　社会主义教育

（3）科学技术是第一生产力　依靠科技进步　提高劳动者素质

（4）"二为"方向　"双百"方针

（5）坚持方向　贯彻方针　总结经验　制定政策

（二）请把下列短文译成外语：

我国本世纪内将为国外发射 30 多颗卫星

【据新华社 11 月 5 日电】　在本世纪内，我国将使用长征火箭为国外发射 30 多颗卫星。

到目前为止，中国长征火箭已有 8 种型号投入使用，并进入国际商业卫星发射服务市场，先后进行了 43 次飞行，成功率高达 87％。中国迄今已发射了 48 颗各类人造地球卫星，其中，中国自行研制的卫星 38 颗，国际用户商业卫星 10 颗。（1996.11.6）

四、小　知　识
BACKGROUND INFORMATION

（一）中国的科技计划和高新技术开发区 China's Programmes for Scientific and Technological Development and Zones for High-

Technological and New-Technical Development

中国国家科技计划共有六个；它们是："攻关（Gōngguān）"计划——即科技攻关计划，开始于 1982 年，内容是选择一批对国民经济具有重大经济效益的科技问题，由国家组织、集中各方面力量进行重点突破。"星火"计划——提出于 1985 年 9 月，内容是向乡镇企业和中小企业推广一批立足地方资源和经济条件的实用技术，带动地方经济的振兴。"火炬（Huǒjù）"计划——从 1988 年开始执行，它致力于高技术研究成果的产业化开发，引导高新技术的起步。"863"计划——即高技术研究发展计划，提出于 1986 年 3 月，所以叫"863"计划。该计划为了在本世纪末、下世纪初增强中国的经济实力，选择了七个对国民经济发展有密切关系的高技术领域作为突破重点。国家科技成果重点推广计划——主要面向农业和传统产业中的大中型骨干企业，推广应用面广、效益显著的重大科技成果。关于基础研究的计划——是探索科学规律，为中国长远科技和经济发展提供后劲的工作。这六大计划体现了中国科技工作面向经济建设主战场，发展高新技术，加强基础研究三个层次的总体战略部署，形成了完整的科技计划体系。

China has six state programmes for scientific and technological development. The first one is 攻关计划 (the Programme for Tackling Key Problems), a short form for "the Programme for Tackling Key Scientific and Technological Problems" which started in 1982. According to this programme, the state organizes some scientists and technologists concerned and pool their wisdom and efforts to tackle the scientific and technological problems which are of great benefits in the national economy. The second one 星火计划 (the Spark Programme) put forward in September 1985 aims at popularizing in the township enterprises and medium and small sized enterprises; new technology based on the local natural resource and economic conditions, so as to promote the development of the local economy. The third one 火炬计划(the Torch Programme) begun in 1988 mainly concerns the industrial application of the achievements in the high technological researches, so as to promote high technology and new technique to progress. The fourth one " 863 计划"（the 863 Programme）is a programme for the development of high technology. So called, because it was set forth in March 1986. It chooses seven high technological fields closely connected with the national economic development as breakthrough points, so as to increase China's economic strength towards the end of this century and the beginning of next century. The fifth one 国家科技成果重点推广计划 (the State Programme for the Wide Utilization of the Important Scientific and Technological Achievements) focuses on the wide utilization of the significant scientific and technological achievements which are extensively applicable and valuable in agriculture and big- or medium-sized key enterprises of the traditional industry. The sixth one 关于基础研究的计划 (the Programme for Basic Scientific and Technological Researches) is set forth to find out scientific laws which will potentially benefit China's long term scientific, technological and economic development. The above-said six programmes outline an overall strategic plan for the main task of economic development, for the development of high technology and new technique and for basic researches that the Chinese scientists and technologists have been undertaking.

国家高新技术产业开发区——它是实施"火炬"计划的重要组成部分和重要基地。从 1988 年国家批准设立北京市新技术产业开发试验区以后，到 1991 年 3 月，共有国家高新技术产业开发区 27

个。

The establishment of the zones for high technological and new technical development as important bases is a part of the Torch Programme. In 1988 the Beijing Zones for Development and Experiment of New Technological Industry was approved by the state. After that and before March 1991，27 development zones of this type were established.

（二）毛泽东《在延安文艺座谈会上的讲话》*Talks at the Yan'an Forum on Literature and Art* by Mao Zedong

毛泽东1942年5月在延安举行的文艺座谈会上的讲话。毛泽东在讲话中全面阐明了中国共产党关于文艺工作的基本观点和方针，是中国文艺工作的指导文献。简称《讲话》。

At the Yan'an Forum on Literature and Art held in May 1942 Mao Zedong gave talks（often abbreviated to《讲话》，*Talks*），generally explaining the Chinese Communist Party's basic viewpoints and policy concerning literature and art. His *Talks* is regarded as a document guiding the work in the literary and artistic fields in China.

（三）"二为"方向和"双百"方针 二为方向（the Direction of Two Services）and 双百方针（the Double-Hundred Policy）

"二为"方向即文艺工作要为人民服务、为社会主义服务。这是中国文艺工作的方向。

二为 is the abbreviated version for "literature and art should serve people and socialism" which is the direction of the work in the literary and artistic fields in China.

"双百"方针即百花齐放、百家争鸣。百花齐放是发展艺术的方法,百家争鸣是发展科学的方法,也就是艺术上的不同形式和风格流派可以自由发展,科学上的不同学派可以自由讨论,以发扬艺术民主和学术民主的方法,促进社会主义科学、文化、艺术的发展和繁荣。

双百 stands for "the policy of letting a hundred flowers blossom and a hundred schools of thought contend". The policy to let a hundred flowers blossom aims to promote the development of art, whereas the policy to let a hundred schools of thought contend is formulated to advance science and technology. In other words, different forms and styles of art can develop freely; and different schools of thought may contend through free discussions. The encouragement of artistic and academic democracy is beneficial to the development and prosperity of socialist science, culture and art.

(四)希望工程 Project Hope

由中国青少年基金会发起的一项捐赠活动,目的是发动社会力量,帮助贫困地区的失学儿童完成小学学业。

This is a donation activity initiated by the Young People's Foundation of China, with the aim of mobilizing the whole society to help drop-out children in poverty-stricken areas finish their studies in primary schools.

(五)"五个一"工程 "Five Ones" Project

即每个省、市、自治区和有关部委党委宣传部每年组织一部好电影、一部好电视剧、一台好戏、一本好书、一篇好文章。自1991年开始实施,1995年增加了一首好歌和一部好广播剧。

This project is for every province, municipality, autonomous region and CPC committee publicity department of ministries and commissions concerned to organize every year one good film, one good TV play, one good drama, one good book and one good article. It started in 1991 and was added in one good song and one good radio play.

（六）中国文艺界的评奖活动 Prizes in Chinese Literary and Artistic Circles

中国文艺界的评奖活动,影响比较大的有:"茅盾文学奖" (Máodùn Wénxuéjiǎng)——是旨在鼓励优秀长篇小说创作的国家级大奖。电影"华表奖"(Huábiǎojiǎng,即原政府奖)——它与"百花奖"(Bǎihuājiǎng)、"金鸡奖"(Jīnjījiǎng)并称为中国电影的三大奖。"华表奖"由广播电影电视部、中宣部、国家教委、解放军总政治部以及全国总工会、团中央、全国妇联等联合组成的评委会评定。"百花奖"——60 年代即已开展的电影评奖活动,以群众投票的方式评定。"金鸡奖"——由电影艺术家评定。电视剧"飞天奖" (Fēitiānjiǎng)——中国电视剧中的大奖。电视剧"金鹰奖" (Jīnyīngjiǎng)——由观众直接投票评定。"梅花奖" (Méihuājiǎng)——戏剧界的评奖活动,评奖对象是优秀中青年演员。文化部"文华奖"(Wénhuájiǎng)——评奖范围是优秀新剧目的创作和演出,目的在于奖掖优秀艺术人才,促进艺术创作和演出的繁荣。

Of the most significant prizes in the Chinese literary and artistic circles, 茅盾文学奖 (the Mao Dun's Literary Prize), a national one, is awarded to successful novelists. 华表奖(the Huabiao Prize, i. e. the former Governmental Prize), one of the three prizes for successful films, is decided by the joint committee of the Bureau of Radio, Film and Television, the Publicity Department of the Central Committee of the Chinese Communist Party, the Ministry of Education, the General Political Department of the People's Liberation Army, the All-China Federation of Trade Unions, the Central Committee of the Chinese Communist Youth League and the National Women's Federation of the People's Republic of China. 百花奖(Hundred Flowers Prize) for outstanding films from the sixties onwards, is decided by the audiences' ballot. 金鸡奖 (the Golden Rooster Prize), another prize for favourable-received films, is decided by a group of film artists. 飞天奖(the Flying Apsaras Prize) is a significant prize for the well received Chinese TV plays. 金鹰奖 (the Golden Eagle Prize) is another prize for the highly-rated TV plays decided by the audiences' ballot. 梅花奖(the Plum Blossom Prize) is awarded to the young or middle-aged outstanding theatrical performers. 文华奖 (the Literary Talent Prize) is given by the Ministry of Culture for the creation and performance of the highly recommended new operas, aiming to encourage good opera writers and performers and to promote the prosperity of opera composition and acting.

第十二课 体 育
XII. SPORTS

一、词语和句子

（一）关于运动会、比赛

1：……运动会 ……赛

---

(1)（标题）第 26 届奥运会隆重开幕　197 个国家和地区
　　10000 多名运动员会聚亚特兰大。（1996.7.21）
(2)（标题）第三届工运会闭幕（1996.10.5）
　　第三届全国农运会在沪开幕。（1996.10.13）
(3)（标题）世界杯女子乒乓球赛开始（1996.9.29）
　　中国羽毛球公开赛揭幕（1996.10.30）
(4) 第八届亚洲青年女子排球锦标赛今天进入第三天，中
　　国队已取得三战三胜的好成绩。（1996.9.19）

2：决赛　半决赛　复赛　预赛

---

(1) 第八届亚洲青年女子排球锦标赛共有 11 支球队参加。每组前两名出线,参加半决赛。半决赛和决赛分别于 20 日和 22 日举行。(1996.9.17)

(2) 根据赛程,12 日进行男女单打 1/8 比赛,13 日进行男女单双打 1/4 比赛,14 日产生女单男双冠军,15 日决出男单女双冠军。(1996.12.12)

(3) 伏明霞(Fú Míngxiá)从预赛到决赛一路领先,最后以超出第二名 40 多分的绝对优势蝉联冠军。(1996.7.29)

(二)关于成绩

1:[打]破/刷新/创造　全国/亚洲/…运动会记录

---

(1) 全国女子举重冠军赛闭幕　七人八次破五项全国记录(1996.10.14)

(2) 安徽选手蔡维艳(Cài Wéiyàn)先后越过 4 米 26 和 4 米 32,两次刷新女子撑竿跳高亚洲记录。原记录 4 米 25 也是由她本人创造的。(1996.10.1)

2：以……成绩，荣获/夺得/获得/……军/……牌

成绩是……

夺冠　居第……　失利/负于……

奖牌　金牌　银牌　铜牌　冠军　亚军

---

(1) 中国体育代表团在本届奥运会上共夺得 50 枚奖牌，
其中金牌 16 枚、银牌 22 枚、铜牌 12 枚。金牌数和奖
牌数均居第四位。(1996.8.5)

(2) 中国体操名将李小双(Lǐ Xiǎoshuāng)以 58.423 分荣
获奥运会体操比赛男子个人全能冠军。(1996.7.28)

(3) 长跑女将王军霞(Wáng Jūnxiá)在女子 5000 米决赛
中，以 14 分 59 秒 88 的成绩战胜所有对手一举夺冠。
(1996.7.30)

(4) 李对红(Lǐ Duìhóng)以明显优势夺冠。获得这个项目
亚军的是保加利亚选手约尔格娃(Yuē'ěrgéwá，
Yorgeva)，成绩是 684.8 环，俄罗斯老将罗格维连科
(Luógéwéiliánkē，Rogevelenko)以 684.2 环获铜牌。
(1996.7.27)

(5) 世界冠军孔令辉(Kǒng Lìnghuī)失利：奥运会乒乓球
男单头号种子、世界冠军孔令辉，今天上午以 1:3 负
于韩国老将金泽珠(Jīn Zézhū，Kim Taek Soo)，未能
进入男单前 8 名。(1996.7.29)

(6) 游泳女将乐靖宜(Lè Jìngyí)在 50 米自由泳比赛中，

仅以百分之三秒负于美国选手,屈居亚军。(1996.7. 28)

（三）生　词

1.	运动会	yùndònghuì	sports meet
2.	…杯	bēi	…cup
3.	乒乓球	pīngpāngqiú	table tennis
4.	羽毛球	yǔmáoqiú	badminton
5.	公开赛	gōngkāisài	open（championship）
6.	揭幕	jiēmù	to ring up the curtain
7.	锦标赛	jǐnbiāosài	championships
8.	决赛	juésài	finals
9.	半决赛	bànjuésài	semi-finals
10.	预赛	yùsài	preliminary trials
11.	排球	páiqiú	volleyball
12.	出线	chūxiàn	to qualify for the next round of competition
13.	赛程	sàichéng	competition schedule or procedure
14.	单/双打	dān/shuāngdǎ	singles/doubles
15.	优势	yōushì	superiority，dominant position
16.	蝉联	chánlián	to continue to hold

(a post or title)

17. 冠军	guànjūn	champion，championship
18. [打]破	[dǎ]pò	to break
19. 刷新	shuāxīn	to break
20. 记录	jìlù	record
21. 举重	jǔzhòng	weightlifting
22. 选手	xuǎnshǒu	athlete player；(selected) contestant
23. 撑竿跳高	chēnggān tiàogāo	pole vault
跳高	tiàogāo	high jump
24. 夺冠	duóguàn	to carry off the prize
25. 失利	shīlì	to suffer a defeat，to lose
26. 负于	fùyú	to lose...to
27. 奖牌	jiǎngpái	medal
…牌	…pái	…medal
28. 亚军	yàjūn	runner-up；second place
29. 体操	tǐcāo	gymnastics
30. 名/女/老将	míng/nǚ /lǎo jiàng	famous/woman/old player
31. 全能	quánnéng	all-round
32. 长跑	chángpǎo	long-distance running
33. 一举	yìjǔ	one action，one stroke
34. 种子[选手]	zhǒngzi [xuǎnshǒu]	seeded player，seed

35. 自由泳　　　zìyóuyǒng　　　free-style swimming
36. 屈居　　　　qūjū　　　　　be forced to accept a place

（四）专有名词

1. 奥[林匹克]运[动]会　Ào[línpǐkè] Yùn[dòng]huì
　　　　　　　　　　　　　the Olympic Games
2. 亚特兰大　　Yàtèlándà　　Atlanta
3. 安徽　　　　Ānhuī　　　　a province in South China
4. 保加利亚　　Bǎojiālìyà　　Bulgaria

二、阅读短文

（一）

第三届全国农民运动会在沪开幕
姜春云代表党中央国务院出席开幕式

本报上海 10 月 12 日电　第三届全国农民运动会今天下午在上海虹口体育场举行了隆重的开幕式。代表党中央、国务院专程前来参加农运会的中央政治局委员、书记处书记、国务院副总理姜春云（jiāng Chūnyún）宣布大会开幕。

开幕式由中国农民体育协会主席肖鹏（Xiāo Péng）主持。组委会主席、上海市市长徐匡迪（Xú Kuāngdí）致欢迎词。中央政治局委员、上海市委书记黄菊（Huáng Jú），全国政协副主席董寅初（Dǒng Yínchū），国家体委主任伍绍祖（Wǔ Shàozǔ）等出席了开幕式。

全国 30 个省市的农民运动员依次（yīcì，successively）进入会场。1800 多名运动员将参加 13 个项目的比赛和表演。（1996.10.13）

1. 虹口体育场　Hóngkǒu Tǐyùchǎng　the Hongkou Stadium
2. 农民体育协会　Nóngmín Tǐyù Xiéhuì　the Peasants Sports Association

（二）

今年最后一项国际乒乓球大赛落幕
中国选手获全部四项冠军

在 今 天 落 幕（luòmù，to ring down the curtain）的 1996 年国际乒联职业巡回赛中，我国乒乓球选手在天津人民体育馆众多观众的加油（jiāyóu，to cheer）声中，一举夺下全部四项冠军。

今天下午进行的男子单打决赛争夺得十分激烈，世界冠军孔令辉迎战（yíngzhàn，to meet，to take on）欧洲乒坛未来之星的萨姆索诺夫（Sàmǔsuǒnuòfū，Samsonov），结果以 3∶1 击败了强硬的对手。女子双打决赛中，中国队邓亚萍（Dèng Yàpíng）和杨影（Yáng Yǐng）第一局以 17∶21 失利，随后三局以 21∶12、21∶16、21∶12 取得最后胜利。男子双打和女子单打冠军于昨天下午产生。中国队一对男双新秀（xīnxiù，new star）王励勤（Wáng Lìqín）和阎森（Yán Sēn）夺冠。女单前四名皆为中国选手，邓亚萍和李菊（Lǐ Jú）分获冠亚军。（1996.12.16）

1. 人民体育馆　Rénmín Tǐyùguǎn　the People's Gymnasium
2. 国际乒[乓球]联[合会]　Guójì Pīng[pāngqiú] Lián[héhuì] the International Table Tennis Federation

三、练 习

(一)熟读下列词语:

(1)奥林匹克运动会 世界大学生运动会 亚洲运动会
全国运动会 工人运动会 农民运动会

(2)锦标赛 邀请赛 公开赛 对抗赛 巡回赛 冠军赛
友谊赛 大奖赛 杯赛 决赛 半决赛 复赛 预赛
四分之一决赛 八分之一赛

(3)奥运会记录 世界记录 亚运会记录 亚洲记录 全国
记录 世界最好成绩 本人最好成绩

(4)打破记录 超过记录 刷新记录 创造记录 平记录
创造最好成绩

(5)荣获冠军 获得亚军 名列第三 退居第四
荣获金牌 荣获桂冠 夺冠 夺魁 卫冕(wèimiǎn,to
protect the crown,to defend one's title) 蝉联 三连冠
夺得银牌 获得铜牌

(6)以 4 分 41 秒 45 的成绩 以 0.01 秒之差(径赛、游泳等
速度类比赛)
比分为 11:2(球类等比赛) 得分为 9.5 分(体操、跳水
等比赛)

(二)请把下列词语填人适当位置:

(金牌 冠军 以 记录 最好成绩 决赛 以…成绩 创
造 退居)

(1)邓亚萍在半决赛中,____21:14、21:10、21:14 的较大优
势击败了香港的齐宝华(Qí Bǎohuá)。____中,她又以3:1
战胜了队友杨影,夺得冠军。(1996.11.26)

(2) 年仅 13 岁的小女孩伏明霞战胜所有对手(duìshǒu,
opponent，adversary)为中国体育代表团夺得第六届世界
游泳锦标赛的首枚____。美国名将威廉斯(Wēiliánsī,
Williams）积分与苏联米罗申娜（Mǐluóshēnnà,
Miroshina)相差 2.64 分,获得季军。比赛中曾一路领先
(yílù lǐngxiān, to lead all the way)的奥运会冠军、中国名
将许艳梅(Xǔ Yànméi)在最后第三个动作中失利,____第
四位。(1991.1.5)

(3) 1986 年 10 月,[女子铅球运动员]隋新梅(Suí Xīnméi)在
全国田径冠军赛上以 18.87 米的成绩获得____。1987
年,隋新梅在第六届全运会上再次投出了 18.87 米的本
人____。1990 年 3 月,隋新梅以 21.10 米的成绩____了
室内女子铅球亚洲____;10 月,第 11 届亚运会上,她终
于____20.55 米的____登上了领奖台(lǐngjiǎngtái,
winner's rostrum or pedestal)最高处。(1991.1.12)

(三)请把下列短文译成外语:

世界无臂蛙王宫宝仁

　　25 岁的无臂青年宫宝仁(Gōng Bǎorén),在今年残疾人奥运
会上夺得 100 米蛙泳的金牌,改写了该项世界记录。十多年来,他
在国内外重大比赛中先后获得 16 枚金牌,5 枚银牌,2 枚铜牌,多
次获得体育道德风尚(fēngshàng, prevailing practice)奖,被国家体
委和中国残联授予优秀运动员奖。尤其是在残奥会上,勇夺金牌,
破世界记录,是他一生中最辉煌(huīhuáng, brilliant, glorious)的
时刻。

　　可又有谁知道,他为此付出了多少心血(xīnxuè, painstaking

effort)和汗水。(1996. 11. 25)

1. 残疾人奥[林匹克]运[动]会　Cánjírén Ào[línpǐkè] Yùn[dòng]huì　the Paralympic Games
2. 中[国]残[疾人]联[合会]　Zhōng[guó] Cán[jírén] Lián[héhuì]　the Chinese Federation for the Disabled

四、小　知　识
BACKGROUND INFORMATION

若干有关体育的简称 Some Useful Abbreviations for Sports and the Organizers

1. 奥委会——奥林匹克委员会（Àolínpǐkè Wěiyuánhuì）the Olympic Committee

   奥运会——奥林匹克运动会（Àolínpǐkè Yùndònghuì）the Olympic Games

   冬奥会、冬季奥运会——冬季奥林匹克运动会（Dōngjì Àolínpǐkè Yùndònghuì）the Winter Olympic Games

2. 全运会——全国运动会（Quánguó Yùndònghuì）the National Games

   冬运会——冬季运动会（Dōngjì Yùndònghuì）the Winter Games

   城运会——全国城市运动会（Quánguó Chéngshì Yùndònghuì）the National Urban Games

   农运会——全国农民运动会（Quánguó Nóngmín Yùndònghuì）the National Farmers' Games

   民运会——全国少数民族传统体育运动会（Quánguó Shǎoshù Mínzú Chuántǒng Tǐyù Yùndònghuì）the National Minority

Traditional Sports Meet

3. 体总——中华全国体育总会（Zhōnghuá Quánguó Tǐyù Zǒnghuì）
All-China Sports Federation

乒协——中国乒乓球协会（Zhōngguó Pīngpāngqiú Xiéhuì）
China Table Tennis Association

排协——中国排球协会（Zhōngguó Páiqiú Xiéhuì）China
Volleyball Association

国际足联——国际足球联合会（Guójì Zúqiú Liánhéhuì）
International Football Federation

国际田联——国际业余田径联合会（Guójì Yèyú Tiánjìng
Liánhéhuì）International Amateur Athletics Federation

亚足联——亚洲足球联合会（Yàzhōu Zúqiú Liánhéhuì）Asian
Football Federation

4. 体坛——体育界（tǐyùjiè）sports circles

排坛——排球界（páiqiújiè）volleyball circles

乒坛——乒乓球界（pīngpāngqiújiè）table tennis circles

田坛——田径界（tiánjìngjiè）athletics circles

泳坛——游泳界（yóuyǒngjiè）swimming circles

羽坛——羽毛球界（yǔmáoqiújiè）badminton circles

5. 男（女）篮——男子（女子）篮球（nánzǐ〈nǚzǐ〉lánqiú）men's
（women's）basketball game；男子（女子）篮球队（nánzǐ〈nǚzǐ〉
lánqiúduì）men's（women's）basketball team

男（女）排——男子（女子）排球（nánzǐ〈nǚzǐ〉páiqiú）men's
（women's）volleyball；男子（女子）排球队（nánzǐ〈nǚzǐ〉
páiqiúduì）men's（women's）volleyball team

男（女）足——男子（女子）足球（nánzǐ〈nǚzǐ〉zúqiú）men's
（women's）football game；男子（女子）足球队（nánzǐ〈nǚzǐ〉
zúqiúduì）men's（women's）football team

6. 男（女）单——男子（女子）单打（nánzǐ〈nǚzǐ〉dāndǎ）men's
   (women's) singles

   男（女）双——男子（女子）双打（nánzǐ〈nǚzǐ〉shuāngdǎ）men's
   (women's) doubles

   混双——男女混合双打（nán nǚ hùnhé shuāngdǎ）mixed
   doubles

7. 三大球——指篮球、排球、足球（lánqiú、páiqiú、zúqiú）
   basketball, volleyball and football

   小球——指羽毛球、乒乓球、网球（yǔmáoqiú、pīngpāngqiú、
   wǎngqiú）等 badminton, table tennis and tennis

第十三课　卫　生
XIII. HEALTH

一、词语和句子

（一）关于卫生事业的发展

医疗条件　防治能力　健康水平　预防为主
中西医并重　婴儿死亡率　人口平均期望寿命

---

(1) 八十年代,我国卫生事业在改革开放中稳步前进,医
疗条件、防治能力、健康水平都得到明显改善和提高。
(1991.4.7.光明)

(2) 我国卫生事业有两个数字特别引人注目,这就是:婴
儿死亡率由建国前的 200‰下降到 31‰;人口平均期
望寿命由 35 岁增加到 70 岁。这些指标显著好于世界
平均水平。(1996.12.10)

(3) 新时期卫生工作的指导方针,是以农村为重点,预防
为主,中西医并重,依靠科技教育,动员全社会参加,
为人民健康服务,为社会主义现代化建设服务。

(1996.12.10)

（二）关于农村卫生事业

合作医疗　医疗预防保健网　乡村医生

(1) 加强农村卫生工作,关键是发展和完善农村合作医疗制度。这是长期实践经验的总结,符合中国国情,符合农民愿望。(1996.12.10)
(2) 合作医疗、农村三级医疗预防保健网和乡村医生是我国农村卫生工作的三大支柱。……要坚持民办公助的原则,筹资应以农民个人投入为主,集体加以扶持。(1996.9.13)

（三）关于中医

中医　中药

(1) 由于我国人口 80% 在农村,中医药是我国防病治病的主要方式。活跃在农村的 100 多万乡村医生,多数能用中西两法防病治病。(1991.1.29)
(2) 既要认真继承中医药的特色和优势,又要勇于创新,积极利用现代科学技术,促进中医药理论和实践的发

148

展,实现中医药现代化,更好地保护和增进人民健康。
(1996.12.10)

(四)关于妇幼保健

> 妇幼保健　防治结合　孕产妇　儿童免疫接种

(1) 新中国成立以来,由于实行防治结合,改善了妇女保健条件,使孕产妇的死亡率由解放初的十万分之一千三百下降到目前的十万分之九十四点七。(1991.1.2)

(2) 儿童计划免疫接种率实现了以乡为单位达到85%,计划免疫针对的几种疾病发病率、死亡率大大降低。(1996.9.28)

(五)生　词

1. 医疗　yīliáo　medical treatment
2. 防治　fángzhì　prevention and cure
3. 预防　yùfáng　to prevent, to take precautions against
4. 婴儿　yīng'ér　infant, baby
5. 死亡率　sǐwánglǜ　death rate, mortality rate

6. 引人注目　yǐn rén zhùmù　noticeable，spectacular

7. 期望　　　qīwàng　　　expectation，expectancy

8. 寿命　　　shòumìng　　life-span，life

　　期望寿命　qīwàng　　　life expectancy
　　　　　　　shòumìng

9. 指标　　　zhǐbiāo　　　target，norm

10. 为主　　　wéizhǔ　　　give first place to

11. 中医　　　zhōngyī　　　traditional Chinese medicine

12. 西医　　　xīyī　　　　western medicine

13. 并重　　　bìngzhòng　　to lay equal stress on

14. 动员　　　dòngyuán　　to mobilize

15. 合作医疗　hézuò yīliáo　cooperative medical service

16. 保健　　　bǎojiàn　　　health care

17. 网　　　　wǎng　　　　network

18. 民办公助　mín bàn　　　to be ran by the local people
　　　　　　　gōng zhù　　and subsidized by the state

19. 筹资　　　chóuzī　　　to raise funds

20. 扶持　　　fúchí　　　　to give aid to，to support

21. 中药　　　zhōngyào　　traditional Chinese medicine

22. 继承　　　jìchéng　　　to inherit，to carry on

23. 创新　　　chuàngxīn　　to blaze new trails，to bring
　　　　　　　　　　　　　forth new ideas

24. 妇幼　　　fùyòu　　　　women and children

25. 孕妇　　　yùnfù　　　　pregnant woman

26. 产妇　　　chǎnfù　　　lying-woman，woman in

		labour
27. 免疫	miǎnyì	immunity
28. 接种	jiēzhòng	to inoculate
29. 针对	zhēnduì	be aimed at
30. 发病率	fābìnglǜ	attack rate of an illness; incidence of a disease

二、阅读短文

（一）

学中医留学生逾万人次

中医药学是我国传统文化的重要组成部分。近十多年来，中医药学逐步被世界认识与接受，有条件的高等中医药院校积极开展了对外教育。据不完全统计，1988 年以后，来华学习中医药的留学生人数达 14700 人次，是 1988 年以前来华学习中医药的留学生总人数的 36 倍。其中本科生 1000 余人，半年以上进修生 5000 余人，各种形式的短期培训生 8000 余人。有些院校还在来华留学生中培养了硕士、博士研究生，或接受了来华进行专向研究的高级进修生。（1996.12.13）

(二)

中国针灸走向世界

如何使中医真正走向世界,是摆在中医界面前的严肃课题(kètí, a question for study)。一位参加世界针灸联合会第四次代表大会的中医专家告诉记者:他们对治疗偏瘫(piāntān, hemiplegia)等疑难杂症(yí nán zázhèng, difficult and complicated cases)很有一套办法,效果也很显著,就是苦于(kǔyú, suffer from a disadvantage)不会外语,难以与外界取得真正的交流。看来,要使中国传统中医走向世界,不仅需要卫生部门的推动,中医工作者也应大力提高自身的综合素质。(1996.9.26)

世界针灸联合会　Shìjiè Zhēnjiǔ Liánhéhuì　the World Federation of Acupuncture and Moxibustion

三、练　习

(一)熟读下列词语:

(1) 医疗条件　卫生条件　保健条件

医疗水平　卫生水平　健康水平

卫生保健　妇幼保健　妇女保健　儿童保健　保健医生

(2) 传染病　常见病　慢性病　多发病　地方病

发病率　死亡率　免疫接种率　人口平均期望寿命

(3) 医疗预防保健网　乡村医生

(4) 中医　中药　针灸

(二)请把下列短文译成外语:

中国人健康指标接近发达国家水平

我国人民的一些主要健康指标已高于发展中国家水平,接近发达国家水平。据联合国儿童基金会(Liánhéguó Értóng Jījīnhuì, United Nations Children's Fund)主编的《世界儿童状况》对中、美、日、印等 11 国统计,我国的平均期望寿命为 70 岁,周岁以下儿童死亡率是 31‰,5 岁以下儿童死亡率为 43‰,在 11 国中分别居第六、第七和第八位,以较低的卫生投入取得了较高的卫生水平。据 1989 年统计,我国千人口医院床位已达 2.33 张、医师 1.44 人、护士 0.84 人;每人年诊疗次数为 2.25 次,对儿童和孕妇逐步开展了系统的保健工作,计划免疫接种率普及到 85% 的县份。(1991.7.14)

四、小 知 识
BACKGROUND INFORMATION

(一)农村三级医疗保健网 The Three-Level Health Care Network

in Chinese Rural Areas

这是中国农村以县、乡（镇）、村三级医疗卫生机构组成的医疗卫生体制；它以县级医疗卫生机构为技术指导中心，以乡镇卫生院为枢纽，以村卫生室为基础。

The Chinese rural medical and health system is a county-town (ship)-village three-level network. The country hospital and health institution function as a guiding centre whereas the township hospital plays a pivotal role among the basic clinics in the villages.

（二）农村合作医疗制度 The Cooperative Medical Service in Rural Areas

这是中国农村互助互济的医疗制度。它是依靠农村集体力量创办起来的，农民就诊时可免收或减收部分费用，从而大大减轻了农民的经济负担，使他们有了基本医疗保障。这一制度六七十年代曾在中国农村广泛推行，在发展中国家产生过巨大影响，世界卫生组织给予了高度评价。

This medical service is of mutual assistance in Chinese rural areas. As it is financed and supported by the farmers, they are entitled to free medical service or only pay reduced charges for the treatment, therefore their financial burden is greatly lightened, and their health basically protected. Measures as such were widely adopted in Chinese rural areas in the 1960s and 1970s, and have produced a great impact in the developing countries. The World Health Organization highly appraised this medical system.

（三）关于数量的几个语素 Some Useful Chinese Morphemes for Words of Quantity

汉语中，关于数量有几个常用的语素，现介绍如下：（括号内的

数字表示第 1 次出现的专题序号)

The following are some useful morphemes for words of quantity (numbers used in the brackets indicate the chapters in which they first appear).

量

总产量(IV)　客运量(IV)　进[/出]口量(IV)　需求量(IV)

水产量(IV)　产量(IV)　总量(IV)　净增量(VII)

[旅客/货物]周转量(VIII)　[污水/废气等]排放量(XV)

森林蓄积量(XV)

值

出口总值(IV)　产值(IV)　增加值(IV)　国民生产总值(V)

国内生产总值(V)

额

货物进[/出]口总额(V)　社会消费零售总额(IX)

储蓄余额(IX)　对外贸易总额(X)　进[/出]口总额(X)

率

文盲率(IV)　已婚率(IV)　离婚率(IV)　增长率(IV)

自给率(IV)　产销率(IV)　普及率(VIII)　通胀率(X)

经济增长率(X)税率(X)　死亡率(XIII)　计划免疫接种率(XIII)

发病率(XIII)　人口出生率(XIV)　自然增长率(XIV)

年增长率(XIV)计划生育率(XIV)　森林覆盖率(XV)

幅

增幅(IV)　　涨幅(IX)

第十四课　人口和人口政策
XIV. POPULATION AND ITS POLICY

一、词语和句子

(一) 关于人口和几个有关的数字

1：人口和总人口

---

(1) 1995 年 10 月 1 日 0 时,全国总人口为 120778 万人。同 1990 年 7 月 1 日 0 时 113368 万人相比,增加了 7410 万人。(1996.2.15,光明)

(2) 截至今年 9 月底,台湾人口已达 2146.99 万,其中男性 1104.012 万,女性为 1042.98 万。(1996.11.22)

2：人口出生率　死亡率　自然增长率

---

(1) 1995 年我国人口出生率为 17.12‰,死亡率为 6.75‰,自然增长率为 10.55‰,全年净增 1271 万

人。(1996.2.16,光明)

(2) 台湾平均出生率为 15‰,死亡率为 5.06‰;都市化程度愈高的县市,出生率愈低,死亡率则是以都市化程度低的县市居高。(1996.11.22)

(3) 香港人口在过去十年间增加了 72 万多人,总数已达到 621.8 万人。在 1986 年至 1991 年间,年增长率为 0.6%,而在 1991 年至 1996 年间,年增长率达到 1.8%。人口增长加快的重要原因是,移居海外的移民不断回流。(1996.11.22)

3:育龄妇女　生育旺盛期　生育峰值年龄

当前正处于第三次人口出生高峰的峰顶,育龄妇女人数、处于生育旺盛期人数和进入生育峰值年龄的妇女人数在"八五"期间将分别比"七五"期间增长 5.5%、16.2%、8.2%。我国人口形势仍然严峻,计划生育任务十分艰巨。(1991.1.28)

(二)关于人口政策

计划生育　国情　基本国策　人均意识　控制人口
人口素质

---

(1) 计划生育是从中国国情和人民切身利益出发的基本国策。(1991.4.8)

(2) 要认真总结贫困地区人口与发展问题的成功经验,把扶贫开发与计划生育更好地结合起来,以促进贫困地区人口与经济社会的协调发展。……尽快改变越穷越生、越生越穷的恶性循环状态,是计划生育的一项长期而艰巨的任务。(1996.10.30)

(3) 要大力进行人口基本国情的教育,要宣传控制人口的重要性和紧迫感,要进一步提高人口素质,要树立"人均意识",把人口工作同整个经济和社会发展目标有机地结合起来。(1990.10.31)

(三)关于计划生育

> 群众路线　宣传教育

(1) 做好计划生育工作,必须坚持群众路线,充分相信群众,依靠群众。(1991.4.29)

(2) [天津市计划生育]把以宣传教育为主,以避孕为主,以经常工作为主的"三为主"方针真正落到实处。(1991.3.3,光明)

(3) 令人兴奋的是,广大群众的生育观念发生了深刻的变化,计划生育、少生优生、优育优教越来越成为广大群众的自觉行动。(1991.3.3)

（四）生 词

1. 出生率	chūshēnglǜ	birth rate
2. 增长率	zēngzhǎnglǜ	growth rate
3. 都市化	dūshìhuà	urbanization
4. 移民	yímín	emigrant，immigrant
5. 回流	huíliú	backflow
6. 育龄	yùlíng	child bearing age
7. 生育	shēngyù	to bear，to give birth to
8. 旺盛期	wàngshèngqī	peak period
9. 峰值	fēngzhí	peak value
10. 高峰	gāofēng	peak，height
11. 峰顶	fēngdǐng	peak，summit
12. 严峻	yánjùn	severe，rigorous，grim
13. 艰巨	jiānjù	arduous，formidable
14. 计划生育	jìhuà shēngyù	family planning
15. 国策	guócè	national policy，the basic policy of a state
16. 意识	yìshi	consciousness
17. 控制	kòngzhì	to control
18. 切身	qièshēn	of immediate concern to oneself，personal
19. 恶性	èxìng	vicious

20. 循环	xúnhuán	circle; to circulate
21. 宣传	xuānchuán	to propagate, to publicize
22. 紧迫感	jǐnpògǎn	sense of urgency
23. 有机地	yǒujīde	organically
24. 群众路线	qúnzhòng lùxiàn	the mass line
25. 避孕	bìyùn	contraception
26. 观念	guānniàn	idea, sense
27. 优生	yōushēng	healthy birth
28. 优育	yōuyù	scientific nurture; good upbringing
29. 优教	yōujiào	excellent or first-rate education

二、阅读短文

（一）

苏州市计划生育成绩显著
人口出生率、自然增长率全省最好

第四次人口普查(pǔchá, general survey or investigation)的资料表明：从 1989 年 7 月 1 日至 1990 年 6 月 30 日，苏州市人口出生率为 14.11‰，自然增长率为 7.66‰，均为江苏省的最好成绩。去年，全市计划生育工作又向前推进了一步，全市人口出生率为 12.75‰，计划生育率为 99.5％。所辖的十个县(市)、区均全面完成了年初与市政府签订的人口指标和计划生育工作目标。

这个市坚持把计划生育纳入经济和社会发展总体规划，在下达经济指标的同时下达人口指标，进一步完善了计划生育目标管理。这个市始终把面向农村、立足基层作为开展计划生育的重点。近年来，逐步健全了基层计生队伍，形成了市、县、乡、村四级计划生育管理网络。（1991.1. 19）

苏州市　Sūzhōu Shì　a city in Jiangsu Province

（二）

全球人口前景依然严峻

本报联合国 5 月 29 日电　联合国人口基金今天发表了 1996 年度《世界人口状况报告》。报告提醒人们：全球人口发展的前景依然十分严峻。

报告显示，目前世界人口的增长速度虽然有所减慢，但仍然很高，每年增加 8600 万人。到 1996 年年中，世界人口将达 58 亿。在 2015 年以前，世界人口还会保持每年 8600 万人以上的增长。预计到 1998 年，世界人口将达 60 亿。

展望今后 20 年，取决于各国的人口政策和采取的行动。在最理想的情况下，世界人口到 2015 年也会达到 71 亿，如果不能有效控制人口增长，世界人口会达到 78 亿。（1996.5.31）

三、练　习

（一）熟读下列词语：

 （1）人口出生率　　人口死亡率　　自然增长率

 （2）人口政策　　　控制人口　　　人口素质

　　　计划生育　　　人均观念　　　人口意识　基本国情
　　　优生　　　　　优育　　　　　优教
　（3）群众路线　　相信群众　　　依靠群众

（二）请把下列短文译成外语：

　　建国 40 年以来，特别是党的十一届三中全会以来，中国的经济发展是比较快的，许多主要产品的产量，如粮食、棉花、煤炭、钢铁、发电量等，都名列世界前列，但是由于人口基数大，按人口平均就排到了世界的后面。到本世纪末，经过艰苦的努力，中国粮食总产量达到 5000 亿公斤，但是由于人口将要增长到 13 亿，人均占有量也只保持现有水平。人均水平上不去，就不能不影响第二步战略的实现，人民生活也很难有较多的改善。因此，一定要进一步增强人口意识和人均观念，把计划生育工作真正放在基本国策的位置上，放在经济和社会发展全局的战略地位。（1991.4.9）

四、小　知　识
BACKGROUND INFORMATION

（一）关于中国人口的几个数据 Some Figures Concerning Chinese Population

　　根据中华人民共和国国家统计局 1990 年 7 月 1 日统计，中国人口的主要数据如下：

　　The following are some figures concerning Chinese population issued on 1st July 1990 by the State Statistical Bureau of the People's Republic of China：

　　中国大陆人口为 1133682501 人。平均每个家庭人数为 3.96

人。性别比(女＝100)：106.6。汉族人口为 1042482187 人，各少数民族人口为 91200314 人。每十万人中各种文化程度的人数为：大学 1422 人，高中 8039 人，初中 23344 人，小学 37057 人，文盲、半文盲(15 岁及 15 岁以上不识字和识字很少的人)占总人口 15.88％。城市人口占总人口 26.33％。人口密度为每平方公里 105 人，超过 500 人的有上海、天津、江苏、北京、山东、河南六个省、市，不足 50 人的有甘肃、内蒙古、新疆、青海、西藏五个省、自治区。0 岁至 14 岁人口占总人口的比重为 27.70％，15 至 59 岁人口为 63.71％，60 及 60 岁以上人口为 8.59％。1989 年育龄妇女平均初育年龄为 23.42 岁，生育高峰年龄为 23 岁，生育率为 242.8‰。

China's mainland population was 1,133,682,501 with an average of 3.96 per household. The sex ratio of women and men was 100 to 106.6. The Hans accounted for 1,042,482,187 whereas the national minorities were 91,200,314. Among every 100,000 people there were 1,422 university students, 8,039 senior middle school pupils, 23,344 junior middle school pupils and 37,057 primary school children. The illiterates and semi-illiterates (of fifteen-year olds and above) made up 15.8％ of the total population. The urban population was 26.33％ of the total. The population density was 105 people per square kilometre in the country as a whole, but Shanghai, Tianjin, Jiangsu, Beijing, Shandong and Henan were as densely populated as over 500 people per square kilometre, whereas Gansu, Nei Monggol (Inner Mongolia), Xinjiang, Qinghai and Tibet had an average of less than 50 people per square kilometre. The age group of 0—14-year olds made up 27.70％ of the total population, the 15——59-year olds amounted to 63.71％ and the 60-year olds and above totalled 8.59％ of all. It was estimated that in 1989 the first child-bearing age of the Chinese women was 23. 42 on an average, that the child-bearing peak age was 23, and that the birth rate was 242. 8‰.

(二)中国的人口和经济发展 China's Population and Its Economic Development

中国的人口 1991 年末为 114333 万人,约占世界人口的 1/5。近 20 年来,由于中国实行计划生育政策,少生了两亿人。中国政府提出:争取今后 10 年平均年人口自然增长率控制在 12. 5‰以内。按照这个目标,到本世纪末的人口总数将不超过 13 亿。

At the end of 1991 China had a population of 1,143,330,000, i. e. one fifth of the world population. In the past 20 years the implementation of the birth-control policy in China resulted in reducing the possible birth of 200 million babies. The Chinese Government is making every effort to limit the annual natural growth of population to 12. 5‰ in the next ten years. Thus China's population will have risen to no more than 1,300 million by the end of this century.

据统计,中国国民收入 1952 年为 589 亿元,1989 年增加到 13125 亿元。按可比价格计算,37 年间增加了 10. 3 倍,平均每年递增 6. 78%。但是,大陆人口从 57482 万人增至 112704 万人,增加了 96%,人均收入只增加了 4. 78 倍。所以,完成中国政府提出的控制人口增长的计划指标,对于保证中国现代化建设第二步、第三步战略目标的实现具有重大意义。

China's national income for 1952 was 58,900 million yuan, but the 1989 figure went up to 1,312,500 million yuan. Compared with the fixed price it rose by 10. 3 times in 37 years with an average annual increase of 6. 78%. During this period the mainland population increased from 574,820,000 to 1,127,040,000, 96%

more than the 1952 figure, but the per capita income was raised by only 4.78 times that of 1952. From the figures indicated above one can see the great significance of the population growth control target set by the Chinese Government. Only by attaining it can the second and third-stage strategic tasks for China's modernization drive be fulfilled.

(三) 世界人口情况 The World Population

世界人口加速增长的趋势十分明显。从 1830 年世界人口达到第 1 个 10 亿,到 1927 年的 20 亿,经历了近一个世纪;从 20 亿到 1960 年的 30 亿,经历了 33 年;从 30 亿到 1974 年的 40 亿,经过了 14 年;从 40 亿到 1987 年的 50 亿,只经过了 13 年。再从 50 亿到 1998 年左右的 60 亿人口,只需 11 年。资料表明,世界人口正以每秒钟 3 人,即每天 25 万人的速度增长。2000 年全世界人口将达 63 亿。

It is obvious that the world population has grown very quickly. In 1830 it was 1,000 million. The increase of another 1,000 million took place in almost one century. 33 years later it was three times that of 1830. But it quickly reached 4,000 million in 1974, and increased to 5,000 million in 1987. By 1998 it is most likely to rise to 6,000 million. The statistical figures show that in every second three babies are born, or the world population goes up by 250,000 daily. By 2000 there will be as many people as 6,300 million in the world.

第十五课　环境保护
XV. ENVIRONMENTAL PROTECTION

一、词语和句子

（一）关于环境保护

污染	水污染	大气污染	噪声
废水	废气	废渣	废物
工业废水	生活污水	固体废物	生活噪声

(1) 环境保护现已成为中国的一项基本国策,其中心内容是预防,同时把环境保护与经济社会发展结合起来。(1991.6.6)

(2) 环境保护是实现可持续发展的关键。作为一个发展中国家,中国始终面临着发展经济和保护环境的双重压力。(1996.9.24)

(3) 从 1996 年开始实施的"九五"计划期间,中国将重点解决污染控制问题,这对扭转水污染、大气污染不断

加剧的趋势,保护公众健康和促进经济增长具有重大意义。(1996.9.13)

(4) 乡镇企业的废水、废气、废渣的排放量,大约占全国总量的 10%。这几年,乡镇企业加强了对污染的处理,使每年污水减少 7 亿吨,废气减少 1200 亿立方米。(1991.3.30)

(5) 1990 年,我国大、中城市大气污染程度依然比较严重。工业废水排放量得到控制,但生活污水排放量增加。城市生活噪声呈上升趋势。工业固体废物排放量比上年稍有下降。(1991.6.5)

(二)关于植树、造林

义务植树　植树造林　绿化　生态环境
森林覆盖率　森林蓄积量

---

(1) 从 1979 年建立基地以来,发动广大职工和家属开展义务植树、绿化、美化环境,目前,绿化面积已达 22.8 万平方米,人均近 90 平方米。植树造林在这里已形成良好的风气。(1996.11.28)

(2) 浙江全省森林蓄积量每年递增 137 立方米,森林覆盖率达 45.8%,名列全国前茅。(1991.3.11)

(3) 我国是个少林国家,森林覆盖率低,全国还有大量宜林荒山、荒滩、荒地没有造上林。林业的现状与发展

国民经济和改善生态环境的要求还不适应,植树造林、绿化祖国的任务十分艰巨。(1991.3.12)

(三)关于野生动物保护

(1) 林业部已决定将面积为 20 万平方公里的藏北羌塘草原建为野生动物自然保护区,这将是世界上最大的"高原珍稀动物园"。(1990.4.15)

(2) 尽管我国野生动物保护工作取得了很大成绩,但破坏野生动物资源现象、捕猎珍稀动物的现象仍然较严重,一些珍稀野生动物面临灭绝的危险。(1991.1.9)

(四)生　　词

1. 污染　　　　　wūrǎn　　　　pollute；pollution

2. 噪声　　　　　zàoshēng　　　noise

3. 废水　　　　　fèishuǐ　　　　waste water，liquid waste

4. 废气　　　　　fèiqì　　　　　waste gas or steam

5. 废渣　　　　　fèizhā　　　　 waste residue

6. 废物　　　　　fèiwù　　　　　waste material，trash

7. 固体　　　　　gùtǐ　　　　　 solid

8. 发展中国家　　fāzhǎnzhōng　developing country
　　　　　　　　guójiā

9. 加剧　　　　　jiājù　　　　　to intensify，aggravate

169

10. 趋势	qūshì	trend，tendency
11. 公众	gōngzhòng	the public
12. 义务	yìwù	volunteer；voluntary
13. 排放量	páifàngliàng	emission or release volume
14. 植树	zhíshù	to plant trees
15. 绿化	lùhuà	to make green by planting trees，flowers，etc.；greening
16. 生态	shēngtài	ecology
17. 森林	sēnlín	forest
18. 覆盖率	fùgàilù	coverage
19. 蓄积量	xùjīliàng	store-up volume
20. 递增	dìzēng	to increase progressively
21. 前茅	qiánmáo	the best，on top
22. 宜林	yílín	to be suitable，to afforest
23. 荒	huāng	waste，barren
24. 滩	tān	beach，sands
25. 野生动物	yěshēng dòngwù	wild animals，wildlife
26. 珍稀	zhēnxī	rare
27. 林业部	línyèbù	ministry of forestry
28. 草原	cǎoyuán	grasslands
29. 高原	gāoyuán	plateau
30. 捕猎	bǔliè	to catch and hunt
31. 灭绝	mièjué	to become extinct

（五）专有名词

1. 浙江 Zhèjiāng a province in East China
2. 藏北 Zàngběi Northern Tibet
3. 羌塘 Qiāngtáng Qangtang (a place in Northern Tibet)

二、阅读短文

（一）

林木护卫(hùwèi, to protect, to guard)京城
首都风沙减少

本报讯 北京市的有林面积突破 1000 万亩大关,达到 1025 万亩,林木覆盖率上升到 36.26％。

60 年代,北京每年大风日数 26.9 天,扬沙日数为 17.2 天。而 1971 年至 1978 年,平均每年的大风日数和扬沙日数分别增加到 36.6 天和 20.5 天。进入 80 年代,平均每年的大风日数和扬沙日数分别降到 18.2 天和 2.34 天。北京的生态环境质量开始向良性(liángxìng, virtuous)转化,有较大的改善。(1996.5.23)

（二）

环保与政绩

什么是真正的政绩（zhèngjì, achievements in one's official career)？重要的一点就是能正确处理经济发展和环境保护的关系，实现经济、环保与社会的协调发展。据悉，河南省明确提出：今后考核（kǎohé, to check, to assess）地方干部政绩重点要看两条，一是经济上去了没有，二是污染下去了没有。如果污染总量没有按规定下去，有关领导不能提拔（tíbá, to promote），有关企业不能评优。愿更多的地方能"以环保论（lùn, to determine）英雄"。（1996.10.11）

河南　　Hénán　　　a province in Central China

三、练　习

（一）熟读下列词语：

   （1）生态环境　　保护生态环境　　改善生态环境
       污染　　　　污染处理　　　　污染程度
       水污染　　　大气污染　　　　噪声污染
       废气　　　　工业废气　　　　废渣　废物　固体废物

废水	工业废水	污水	生活污水

(2) 植树　　　　植树造林　　　义务植树
　　绿化　　　　绿化造林　　　绿化祖国
　　森林资源　　森林覆盖率　　林木覆盖率　森林蓄积量
(3) 野生动物　　珍稀动物　　　珍稀濒危动物
　　野生动物保护区　　　　　　自然保护区

（二）请把下列短文译成外语：

(1)

高尔夫与环保

据不完全统计，目前我国已建成和正在建的高尔夫（gāo'ěrfū，golf）球场达百余个。不少外商对此项投资很感兴趣。然而，高尔夫球场所带来的环境问题却很少有人注意。

专家指出，今后我国在审批（shěnpī，to examine and approve）高尔夫球场建设项目时，一要严格坚持利用荒地、不占耕地（gēngdì，cultivated land）原则；二要重视环境评估（pínggū，assessment），减少和避免生态破坏及污染，使高尔夫球真正成为"绿色运动"。（1996.10.11）

(2)

1996年3月5日，第八届全国人大第四次会议审议通过了《关于国民经济和社会发展"九五"计划和2010年远景目标纲要》，把科教兴国和可持续发展作为两项基本战略，并提出："到2000年，力争使环境污染和生态破坏加剧的趋势得到基本控制，部分城市和地区的环境质量有所改善。"到2010年，基本改变生态恶化的状况，城乡环境有比较明显的改善。（1996.9.13）

四、小 知 识
BACKGROUND INFORMATION

(一)中国的植树节 China's Tree-Planting Day

中国的植树节是 3 月 12 日。在每年的这一天或这一天的前后,中国都要开展全国范围的义务植树活动。

中国的全民义务植树活动始于 1981 年。这年的 12 月 13 日,五届人大四次会议根据邓小平的倡议,通过了《关于开展全民义务植树运动的决议》。《决议》规定每个适龄公民每年义务植树 3 至 5 株。10 年来,全国参加义务植树的人数达 20 亿人次,义务植树 100 亿株。

It takes place on 12th March. Around this day the people all over China voluntarily plant trees. The Tree-Planting Day, as officially prescribed by the Government, started in 1981. In the Fourth Session of the Fifth National People's Congress held on 13th December, a resolution concerning nationwide tree-planing was adopted. According to that, it is voluntary for every citizen of the right age to plant 3—5 trees each year. In the past ten years 2,000 million people-times were involved and 10,000 million trees were planted.

(二)"三北"防护林体系和中国林业的重点工程 The Shelterbelts in "the Three Northern Regions" and the Key Projects of the Chinese Forest Industry

"三北"指中国东北、华北、西北地区。除了"三北"防护林体系

174

以外,中国林业重点工程还有:速生丰产用材林基地、长江上游防护林体系、沿海防护林体系、平原农田防护林体系等。

"The Three Northern Regions" stands for the northwest, northern and northeast parts of China. Apart from the shelterbelts in "the Three Northern Regions", there are also the following key forest projects: quickly-growing timber forest bases, the shelterbelts along the upper reaches of the Yangtze River, the coastal shelterbelts and the shelterbelts on plain farmland.

(三)中国的土地面积计量单位:亩(mǔ) Chinese Unit of Measurement for Area:亩(mǔ)

在关于中国农业产量的报道中,常常可看到"亩产"一词,意思是每一亩农田的产量。长期以来,中国土地面积计量单位沿用"[市]顷"(shìqǐng)、"[市]亩"(shìmǔ)、"[市]分"(shìfēn)、"[市]厘"(shìlí)等,一顷等于一百亩,一亩等于十分,一分等于十厘;一顷等于6.6667公顷,一亩等于1/15公顷。这样的计量单位叫做"市制"(shìzhì)。为便于跟国际接轨,中国国家技术监督局、国家土地管理局、农业部联合通知,自1992年1月1日起,在统计工作和对外签约中,一律使用规定的计量单位:平方公里(km²,等于100万平方米)、公顷(ha,1万平方米)、平方米(m²)。

亩产 (yield per *mu*) can often be found in the reports about China's agricultural yield, meaning the yield of per *mu* farmland. For a long time the Chinese system of measurement known as 市制 has been used in China. One (市)顷 is equal to 100 *mu*, or 6.6667 hectares. One *mu* is equal to ten *fen* (分), or 1/15 hectare. One *fen* is equal to ten *li* (厘). In order to keep up with the international system, the China State Bureau of Technical Supervision, the State Bureau of Land Administration and the

Ministry of Agriculture jointly sent out a notice in which square kilometre (km^2, or one million square metres), hectare (ha, or 10,000 square metres) and square metre (m^2) are prescribed as the standard measurements for statistics and contract writing.

第十六课　国　　际
XVI. INTERNATIONAL AFFAIRS

一、词语和句子

（一）关于中外关系

1：同……建立/发展/加强/改善/恢复……关系
外交关系　　友好合作关系　　睦邻友好关系
战略关系

---

(1) 中国既向发达国家开放,也向发展中国家开放,在平
等互利的基础上积极开展广泛的国际合作,促进共同
发展。(1996.9.20)

(2) 中国奉行独立自主的和平外交政策,不同任何大国结
盟和建立战略关系。中国愿意在和平共处五项原则基
础上发展同世界各国的友好合作关系。(1991.5.18)

(3) 中国重视同周边国家发展睦邻友好关系。……中国同
印度尼西亚共和国恢复了外交关系,同新加坡共和国

建立了外交关系,为我国发展同这两个国家的友好关系开辟了广阔的前景。(1991.5.18)

(4) 希望中日两国官方和民间共同努力,把中日关系不断推向前进,使中日两国世世代代友好下去。(1991.8.9)

2:为……作出……　为……而……

国际社会　国际政治新秩序　国际经济新秩序

世界和平　人类进步

---

(1) 中国愿意同国际社会一道,为尽早全面、公正和合理地政治解决柬埔寨问题而努力。(1991.5.8)

(2) 我们要发展同世界各国的友好关系,同各国人民一道,为建立国际政治新秩序和经济新秩序,维护世界和平,促进人类进步事业,做出应有的贡献。(1991.1.2)

3:独立自主　和平共处五项原则　和平外交政策

霸权主义　强权政治

---

(1) 我们要继续奉行独立自主的和平外交政策,反对霸权主义和强权政治……(1991.1.2)

（2）（标题）刘华清（Liú Huáqīng）同希拉克（Xīlākè，
　　　Chirac）会见　指出中国执行的是防御性国防政策，
　　　不威胁任何国家（1996.9.15）

（3）在新型的国际关系中，必须严格遵守和平共处五项原
　　　则。（1991.4.25）

（4）只要这些[建立区域组织和集团的]主张有利于促进
　　　世界经济发展，有利于各国各地区加强经济贸易交流
　　　和合作，而不是排斥其他国家和地区，我们都是赞赏
　　　的。（1991.6.13，光明）

（二）关于国际关系

> 在……基础上　以……为基础
> 协商解决　一律平等

（1）国际新秩序应该建立在所有国家不分大小强弱，一律
　　　平等和互不干涉内政的基础上，国际事务应由各国协
　　　商解决，而不应由一两个大国垄断。（1991.1.8）

（2）钱其琛外长建议各国在互相尊重主权和领土完整、互
　　　不侵犯、互不干涉内政、和平共处的原则基础上建立
　　　和发展政治、外交和经济关系。（1991.1.27）

（3）要谈国际新秩序，必须是同过去那种以霸权主义和强
　　　权政治为基础的旧秩序相区别，应该是一种崭新的关
　　　系。

（4）中、俄、英、法、美五个常任理事国外长今天在联合国总部联合发表声明。声明重申他们对联合国的承诺，对世界各地区的冲突表示深切关注，对联合国在维护国际和平与安全等方面所作的工作表示赞赏。（1996.9.28）

（三）生　　词

1. 奉行	fèngxíng	to pursue（a policy，etc.）
2. 和平	hépíng	peace
3. 结盟	jiéméng	to form an alliance
4. 共处	gòngchǔ	to coexist；coexistence
5. 睦邻	mùlín	good-neighbourliness
6. 前景	qiánjǐng	prospect
7. 官方	guānfāng	official，of the government
8. 世世代代	shìshìdàidài	from generation to generation
9. 一道	yídào	together，alongside
10. 维护	wéihù	to defend，to maintain
11. 致力	zhìlì	to devote oneself to，to work for
12. 赞赏	zànshǎng	to appreciate，to admire
13. 霸权主义	bàquán zhǔyì	hegemonism
14. 强权政治	qiángquán zhèngzhì	power politics

15. 防御	fángyù	to defend，to guard
16. 国防	guófáng	national defence
17. 威胁	wēixié	to threaten，to menace
18. 区域	qūyù	region，area
19. 排斥	páichì	to exclude，to repel
20. 干涉	gānshè	to interfere，to intervene
21. 事务	shìwù	affairs
22. 垄断	lǒngduàn	to monopoly
23. 主权	zhǔquán	sovereign rights，sovereignty
24. 完整	wánzhěng	complete，integrated
25. 侵犯	qīnfàn	to violate，to infringe upon
26. 常任理事国	chángrèn lǐshìguó	permanent member state of a council
27. 总部	zǒngbù	headquarters，head office
28. 承诺	chéngnuò	to promise，to undertake
29. 关注	guānzhù	to pay close attention to，to follow with interest

（四）专有名词

1. 印度尼西亚	Yìndùníxīyà	Indonesia
2. 新加坡	Xīnjiāpō	Singapore
3. 柬埔寨	Jiǎnpǔzhài	Cambodia

二、阅读短文

（一）

世界人民都希望和平与发展

　　江泽民指出,如果各国都能以和平共处五项原则来处理相互关系,世界上许多冲突都可以得到避免和解决。

　　他向客人们介绍了中国关于在和平共处五项原则基础上建立国际政治、经济新秩序的主张,他说,处理国家之间的关系要根据和平共处五项原则,其中最重要的一点是互不干涉内政,由各国人民自己来决定自己的社会制度。不同的社会制度和意识形态不应影响国与国之间正常关系的发展。他说,世界人民都希望和平与发展,这是当代的主要潮流。(1991.12.11,海外)

(二)

日中关系讨论会在东京举行

　　据新华社东京 12 月 14 日电　日本各界人士 130 多人今天在此间日中友好会馆举行日中关系讨论会。与会者一致认为,巩固和发展面向 21 世纪的日中友好合作关系不仅符合两国人民的利益,而且对亚洲地区的稳定与繁荣都是必不可少的。

　　与会者认为,两国在 1972 年实现邦交正常化时发表的日中联合声明和 1978 年签订的日中和平友好条约,是两国发展友好合作关系的根本,日中双方应本着这两个文件的精神处理影响两国关系正常发展的问题。(1996.12.16)

三、练　习

(一)熟读下列词语:

(1) 建立关系　发展关系　加强关系　改善关系　恢复关系
外交关系　友好关系　睦邻关系　战略关系

(2) 国际社会　发达国家　发展中国家
国际新秩序　国际政治新秩序　国际经济新秩序
强权政治　霸权主义

(3) 和平外交政策　和平共处五项原则

　　互相尊重主权和领土完整　互不侵犯　互不干涉内政

　　平等互利　和平共处

(4) 积极的努力　自己的努力　应有的努力

　　积极的贡献　自己的贡献　应有的贡献

(二)请把下列短文译成外语：

(1) 近几年来,世界形势发生了巨大的变化,战后四十多年形成的旧格局已经打破,新的格局正在形成。中国是一个发展中的社会主义国家,需要一个长时期的国际和平环境,以更好地进行现代化建设。怎样创造这样一个良好的环境,我认为,就是坚持独立自主的和平外交政策,坚持和平共处五项原则。(1991.3.28)

(2) 中国认为,未来的国际政治经济新秩序应该建立在和平共处五项原则的基础上。由一个国家和几个国家领导全世界,将是很危险的。我们认为,世界上所有的国家不分大小、贫富、强弱,都是世界大家庭中平等的一员,对世界和平与发展既享有平等的权利,也有各自应尽的义务。(1991.6.13)

小　知　识
BACKGROUND INFORMATION

(一)和平共处五项原则 Five Principles of Peaceful Coexistence

　　简称"五项原则"。它们是:互相尊重主权和领土完整,互不侵犯,互不干涉内政,平等互利,和平共处。这五项原则在 1954 年中国和印度《关于中国西藏地方和印度之间的通商和交通协定》中第一次提出。同年 6 月,中国和印度、中国和缅甸总理分别在他们的联合声明中重申并确认这五项原则是国际关系的指导原则。五项原则已为许多国家接受,被认为是处理国与国之间关系的基本准则。

It is abbreviated to "Five Principles", i. e. mutual respect for each other's territorial integrity and sovereignty; mutual non-aggression; mutual non-interference in each other's internal affairs; equality and mutual benefit; peaceful coexistence. These Five Principles were first put down in the Agreement on Trade and Intercourse between China's Tibet and India in 1954. In their joint statements respectively concluded in June the same year, the Chinese, Indian and Burmese Premiers affirmed and reaffirmed the Five Principles as the guide to the international relations. Now the Five Principles have been widely accepted and are regarded as the basic principles guiding the relations between one country and another.

(二)若干区域组织和集团及其简称 Some Regional Organizations and Groups and Their Abbreviations

阿盟——阿拉伯国家联盟:1945 年 3 月签订《阿拉伯国家联盟公约》,联盟正式成立。

阿盟——阿拉伯国家联盟 League of Arab States (LAS):It was formally organized after the conclusion of the Pact of the League of Arab States in March 1945.

安第斯集团——成立于 1969 年,由玻利维亚、哥伦比亚、厄瓜多尔、秘鲁和委内瑞拉五国组成。1991 年 12 月五国总统协议 1992 年 1 月 1 日成立安第斯自由贸易区。

安第斯集团 Andean Group:It was formed by Bolivia,

Colombia，Ecuador，Peru and Venezuela in 1969. The presidents of the five countries reached an agreement in December 1991. As a result the Andean Free Trade Zone was formed on 1st January 1992.

北约——北大西洋公约组织:《北大西洋公约》签订于 1949 年 4 月。1949 年 8 月,条约生效时,成立了北大西洋公约组织。

北约—— 北大西洋公约组织 North Atlantic Treaty Organization (NATO)：The Treaty was signed in April 1949. The Organization came into being after the Treaty became effective in August 1949.

不结盟运动——不结盟国家和政府首脑会议:成立于 1961 年 9 月。

不结盟运动—— 不结盟国家和政府首脑会议 Non-Aligned movement：The Conference of Heads of State and Government of the Non-Aligned Countries began in September 1961.

东盟——东南亚国家联盟:1976 年 8 月成立。成员有:印度尼西亚、泰国、菲律宾、新加坡、马来西亚等国。

东盟—— 东南亚国家联盟 Association of Southeast Asian Nations (ASEAN)：It was founded in August 1976. Its member states are Indonesia，Thailand，the Philippines，Singapore and Malaysia.

非统——非洲统一组织:非洲独立国家组成的区域性组织,成立于 1963 年 5 月。

非统—— 非洲统一组织 Organization of African Unity (OAU)：It is a regional organization formed by some independent African countries in May 1963.

海湾合作委员会——海湾阿拉伯国家合作委员会:波斯湾的巴林、科威特、阿曼、卡塔尔、沙特阿拉伯和阿拉伯联合酋长国 6 个阿拉伯国家组成,1981 年 5 月成立。

海湾合作委员会——海湾阿拉伯国家合作委员会 Gulf Cooperation Council for the Arab States：It was formed in May 1981 by six Persian Gulf Arab States of Bahrain，Kuwait，Oman，Qatar，Saudi Arabia and the United Arab Emirates.

里约集团——里约热内卢集团:成立于 1986 年 12 月 18 日,现有阿根廷、玻利维亚、巴西、智利、哥伦比亚、厄瓜多尔、墨西哥、巴拉圭、秘鲁、乌拉圭、委内瑞拉、哥斯达黎加、牙买加等 13 个成员国。

里约集团——里约热内卢集团 Rio de Janeiro Group：It was formed on 18th December 1986. Its member states are Argentina，Bolivia，Brazil，Chile，Colombia，Ecuador，Mexico，Paraguay，Peru，Uruguay，Venezuela，Costa Rica and Jamaica.

南锥体共同市场(南方共同市场):阿根廷、巴西、巴拉圭、乌拉圭 4 个南美国家 1991 年 3 月 26 日签约建立南锥体共同市场。

南锥体共同市场(南方共同市场) Southern Cone Common Market (Southern Common Market) — On 26th March 1991 the south American countries of Argentina，Brazil，Paraguay and Uruguay jointly signed an agreement concerning the organization of the South Cone Common Market.

欧安会——欧洲安全和合作会议:第一次首脑会议于 1975 年 7—8 月举行,参加会议的有欧洲 31 国以及美国、加拿大、土耳其、塞浦路斯等 35 国。

欧安会——欧洲安全和合作会议 Conference on Security and Cooperation in Europe (CSCE)：The first summit conference was hold from July to August 1975，and attended by 31 European countries and the United States，Canada，Turkey and Cyprus.

欧共体——欧洲共同体:1965 年 4 月签约,1967 年 7 月成立。

现有成员国 12 国。

欧共体——欧洲共同体 European Community（EC）：The Agreement of its formation was concluded in April 1965，and its formation took place in July 1967. At present there are 12 member states.

欧佩克（OPEC）——石油输出国组织：成立于 1960 年 9 月。参加者都是亚、非、拉石油生产国。

欧佩克——石油输出国组织 Organization of Petroleum Exporting Countries（OPEC）：It was set up in September 1960. Its members are Asian，African and Latin American oil-producing countries.

欧洲共同市场——又称"欧洲经济共同体"、"西欧共同市场"，1957 年 3 月签订《欧洲经济共同体条约》，1958 年 1 月成立。1975 年 5 月同中国建立正式关系。

欧洲共同市场 European Common Market（ECM）— Also known as "the European Economic Community" or "the Common Market". The Treaty of the European Economic Community was concluded in March 1957，and the Market was formed in January 1958. The formal relations were established between China and ECM in May 1975.

欧洲自由贸易联盟——成立于 1960 年 5 月。现有成员为挪威、葡萄牙、瑞士、瑞典、奥地利、芬兰、冰岛等 7 国。

欧洲自由贸易联盟 European Free Trade Association（EFTA）：It was set up in May 1960. At present its member states are Norway，Portugal，Switzerland，Sweden，Austria，Finland and Iceland.

七十七国集团——成立于 1964 年，1989 年 6 月有成员国 128 个。

七十七国集团 Group of 77：It was formed in 1964. Up to June 1989 there were as many as 128 member states.

伊斯兰会议——1971 年 5 月成立的伊斯兰国家组织，成员国都是信奉伊斯兰教的国家和地区。

伊斯兰会议 Islamic Conference：It was organized by the Moslems countries or regions in May 1971.

亚太经合组织——亚洲和太平洋区域经济合作组织：成立于 1989 年。共有 18 个成员。

亚太经合组织——亚洲和太平洋区域经济合作组织 Asian-Pacific Economic Cooperation (APEC)：Formed in 1989，it has 18 members.

生词总表
VOCABULARY
（按汉语拼音字母顺序排列）

196

责任编辑 贾寅淮
封面设计 安洪民

图书在版编目(CIP)数据

新闻汉语导读/施光亨,王绍新编著;熊文华,梁骁英文翻译.—
北京:华语教学出版社,1998.9
ISBN 7-80052-633-X

I. 新… II.①施… ②王… ③熊… ④梁… III.新闻—对外汉语
教学—阅读—教材 IV.H195.4

中国版本图书馆 CIP 数据核字(98)第 17287 号

新闻汉语导读

编 著 施光亨 王绍新
英文翻译 熊文华 梁 骁

*

ⓒ华语教学出版社
华语教学出版社出版
(中国北京百万庄路 24 号)
邮政编码 100037
中国电影出版社印刷厂印刷
中国国际图书贸易总公司发行
(中国北京车公庄西路 35 号)
北京邮政信箱第 399 号 邮政编码 100044
1998 年(大 32 开)第一版
(汉英)
ISBN 7-80052-633-X/H · 732(外)
01650
9-CE-3296P